simple
thai &
chinese
step-by-step

THUNDER BAY
P·R·E·S·S

San Diego, California

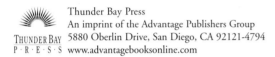

Thunder Bay Press
An imprint of the Advantage Publishers Group
5880 Oberlin Drive, San Diego, CA 92121-4794
www.advantagebooksonline.com

The Foundry, 8035 Enterprise Street, Burnaby, BC V5A 1V7, U.K.

ISBN 1-57145-745-3

Library of Congress Cataloging-in-Publication Data available upon request.

Printed in Korea.

1 2 3 4 5   06 05 04 03 02

ACKNOWLEDGMENTS

Authors: Catherine Atkinson, Juliet Barker, Liz Martin, Carol Tennant, Mari Mererid Williams, and Elizabeth Wolf-Cohen
Editorial Consultant: Gina Steer
Project Editor: Karen Fitzpatrick
Photography: Colin Bowling and Paul Forrester
Home Economists and Stylists: Jacqueline Bellefontaine, Mandy Phipps, Vicki Smallwood, and Penny Stephens
Design Team: Helen Courtney, Jennifer Bishop, Lucy Bradbury, and Chris Herbert

All props supplied by Barbara Stewart at Surfaces.

NOTE
Recipes using uncooked eggs should be avoided by infants,
the elderly, pregnant women, and anyone with a compromised immune system.

Special thanks to everyone involved in this book, particularly Karen Fitzpatrick and Gina Steer.

CONTENTS

SOUPS & STARTERS

FISH & SHELLFISH

MEAT

POULTRY

VEGETABLES

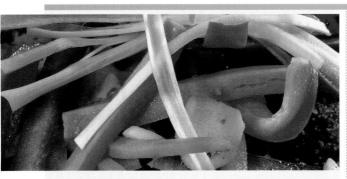

ENTERTAINING

CLEANLINESS IN THE KITCHEN

It is well worth remembering that many foods can carry some form of bacteria. In most cases, the worst it will lead to is a bout of food poisoning or gastroenteritis, although for certain groups this can be more serious—the risk can be reduced or eliminated by good hygiene and proper cooking.

Do not buy food that is past its sell-by date, and do not consume any food that is past its use-by date. When buying food, use your eyes and nose. If the food has a bad color or a rank, acrid, or simply bad smell, do not buy or eat it under any circumstances.

Take special care when preparing raw meat and fish. A separate chopping board should be used for each; wash the knife, board, and your hands thoroughly before handling or preparing any other food.

Regularly clean, defrost, and clear out your refrigerator or freezer—it is worth checking the packaging to see exactly how long each product is safe to freeze.

Avoid handling food if suffering from an upset stomach, as bacteria can be passed through food preparation.

Dishtowels must be washed and changed regularly. Ideally, use disposable paper towels that can be discarded after use. More durable cloths should be left to soak in bleach, then washed in the washing machine in hot water.

Keep your hands, cooking utensils, and food preparation surfaces clean, and do not allow pets to climb onto any work surfaces.

BUYING

Avoid bulk buying where possible, especially of meat, poultry, fish, fruit, and vegetables, unless buying to store in the freezer. Fresh foods lose their nutritional value rapidly, so buying a little at a time minimizes loss of nutrients. It also eliminates a packed refrigerator, which can reduce the effectiveness of the refrigeration process.

When buying prepackaged goods, such as cream and yogurt, check that the packaging is intact and not damaged or pierced at all. Cans should not be dented, pierced, or rusty. Check the sell-by dates for cans and packets of dry ingredients, such as flour and rice, as well. Store fresh foods in the refrigerator as soon as possible—don't leave in your car.

When buying frozen foods, ensure that they are not heavily iced on the outside and that the contents feel completely frozen. Ensure that the frozen foods have been stored at the correct storage level and that the temperature is below 0° F. Bring home and place in the freezer as soon as possible after purchase.

PREPARATION

Make sure that all work surfaces and utensils are clean and dry. Hygiene should be given priority at all times.

Separate chopping boards should be used for raw and cooked meats, fish, and vegetables. Currently, a variety of good-quality plastic boards come in various designs and colors. This makes differentiating easier, and the plastic has the added hygienic advantage of being washable at high temperatures in the dishwasher. If using the board for fish, first wash in cold water, and then in hot water to prevent odor. Also, remember that knives and utensils should always be cleaned thoroughly after use.

When cooking, be particularly careful to keep cooked and raw food separate to avoid any contamination. It is worthwhile to wash all fruits and vegetables, regardless of whether they are going to be eaten raw or lightly cooked. This rule should apply even to prewashed herbs and salads.

Do not reheat food more than once. If using a microwave, always check that the food is piping hot all the way through. In theory, the food should reach 160° F, and needs to be cooked at that temperature for at least three minutes to ensure that all bacteria are killed.

All frozen poultry must be thawed thoroughly before using, including chicken and game hen. Remove the food to be thawed from the freezer and place in a shallow dish to contain the juices. Leave the food in the refrigerator until it is thawed completely. A 3-lb. whole chicken will take about 26 to 30 hours to thaw. To speed up the process, immerse the chicken in cold water. However, make sure that the water is changed regularly. When the joints move freely and no ice crystals remain in the cavity, the bird is thawed.

Once thawed, remove the wrapper and pat the chicken dry. Place the chicken in a shallow dish, cover lightly, and store as close to the base of the refrigerator as possible. The chicken should be cooked as soon as possible.

Some foods can be cooked from frozen, including many prepacked foods such as soups, sauces, casseroles, and breads. Where applicable follow the manufacturer's instructions.

Vegetables and fruits can also be cooked from frozen, but meats and fish should be thawed first. The only time food can be refrozen is when the food has been thawed thoroughly, then cooked. Once the cooked food has cooled, it can be frozen again. On such occasions the food can only be stored for one month.

All poultry and game (except for duck) must be cooked thoroughly. When cooked, the juices will run clear from the thickest part of the bird—the best area to try is usually the thigh. Other meats, like ground meat and pork, should be cooked all the way through. Fish should turn opaque, be firm in texture, and break easily into large flakes.

When cooking leftovers, make sure they are reheated until piping hot and that any sauce or soup boils first.

STORING
REFRIGERATING AND FREEZING

Meat, poultry, fish, seafood, and dairy products should all be refrigerated. The temperature of the refrigerator should be between 34–41° F, while the freezer temperature should not rise above 0° F.

To ensure the optimum refrigerator and freezer temperature, avoid leaving the door open for a long time. Try not to overstock the refrigerator, as this reduces the airflow inside and reduces the effectiveness of the cooling system.

When refrigerating cooked food, let it cool completely before refrigerating. Hot food will raise the temperature of the refrigerator and possibly affect, or spoil, other food stored inside.

Food within the refrigerator and freezer should always be covered. Raw and cooked food should be stored in separate parts of the refrigerator. Cooked food should be kept on the top shelves of the refrigerator, while raw meat, poultry, and fish should be placed on bottom shelves to avoid drips and cross-contamination. It is recommended that eggs should be refrigerated in order to maintain their freshness and shelf life.

Take care that frozen foods are not stored in the freezer for too long. Blanched vegetables can be stored for one month; beef, lamb, poultry, and pork for six months; and unblanched vegetables and fruits in syrup for a year. Oily fish and sausages can be stored for three months. Dairy products can last four to six months, while cakes and pastries can be kept in the freezer for three to six months.

HIGH-RISK FOODS

Certain foods may carry risks to people who are considered vulnerable, such as the elderly, the ill, pregnant women, babies, young infants, and those suffering from a recurring illness.

It is advisable to avoid those foods listed below, which belong to a higher-risk category.

There is a slight chance that some eggs carry the bacteria salmonella. Cook the eggs until both the yolk and the white are firm to eliminate this risk. Pay particular attention to dishes and products incorporating lightly cooked or raw eggs, which should be eliminated from the diet. Sauces such as hollandaise and mayonnaise, mousses, soufflés, and meringues all use raw or lightly cooked eggs, as do custard-based dishes, ice creams, and sorbets. These are all considered high-risk foods to the vulnerable groups mentioned above.

Certain meats and poultry also carry the potential risk of salmonella and so should be cooked thoroughly until the juices run clear and there is no pinkness left. Unpasteurized products, such as milk, cheese (especially soft cheese), pâté, and meat (both raw and cooked) all have the potential risk of listeria and should be avoided.

When buying seafood, buy from a reputable source that has a high turnover to ensure freshness. Fish should have bright, clear eyes, shiny skin, and bright pink or red gills. The fish should feel stiff to the touch, with a slight smell of sea air and iodine. The flesh of fish steaks and fillets should be translucent with no signs of discoloration. Mollusks, such as scallops, clams, and mussels, are sold fresh and are still alive. Avoid any that are open or do not close when tapped lightly. In the same way, univalves should withdraw back into their shells when prodded lightly. When choosing cephalopods, such as squid and octopus, they should have a firm flesh and pleasant sea smell.

As with all fish, care is required when freezing. It is imperative to check whether the fish has been frozen before. If it has been frozen, then it should not be frozen again under any circumstances.

FRESH INGREDIENTS

Thai and Chinese cooking are among the world's greatest. In both, the basic philosophy of balance is the same; the freshest produce is combined with the flavors of dried, salted, and fermented ingredients, preserves, and condiments. Most ingredients are now available in ordinary supermarkets and a few of the more unusual ones in Asian or Chinese markets.

BABY CORN

These tiny, tender cobs of corn, about 3 in. long, add a crunchy texture and sweet flavor to many dishes. When buying, make sure that they are bright yellow, with no brown patches, and are firm and crisp.

BAMBOO SHOOTS

Bamboo shoots are young, creamy-colored, conical-shaped shoots of edible bamboo plants. They add a crunchy texture and a clean, mild flavor to many dishes, and are available in Chinese groceries, as well as in most supermarkets.

BASIL

Holy basil with small, dark leaves and purple stalks is frequently used in Thai cooking, although sweet basil, more easily obtainable in grocery stores, may be used instead. If you have bought more basil than needed, wrap the extra leaves in barely damp paper towels. Place in a plastic bag, and store in the refrigerator for up to 4 days. Alternatively, place a bunch of basil in a glass of water. Place a plastic bag over the leaves and refrigerate for up to one week, replacing the water every two days.

BEAN SPROUTS

These are the shoots of the mung bean and are readily available in the produce section of most supermarkets. They contribute a wonderfully crisp texture when added to stir-fries.

BLACK BEANS

These small, black soybeans are also known as "salted black beans," as they have been fermented with salt and spices. Sold loose in Chinese stores, but also available canned, they have a rich flavor and are often used with ginger and garlic, with which they have a particular affinity. So important is the soybean in Chinese cooking, it is considered one of the five sacred grains.

BOK CHOY

The most common variety has long, slightly ridged, white stems like celery and large, oval, thick, dark-green leaves. Bok choy has a mild, fresh, slightly peppery taste, and needs very little cooking. Choose smaller ones if possible, as they are more tender. Store in the bottom of the refrigerator.

CHILIES

There are many different kinds of chilies and generally, the smaller they are, the more fierce the heat. Red chilies are generally milder than green ones because they sweeten as they become riper. Thai cooks often include the seeds in cooking, but to moderate the heat, scrape out and discard the seeds.

CHINESE CABBAGE

Chinese cabbage looks like a large, tightly packed lettuce with crinkly, pale-green leaves. Imports from Israel, Spain, Holland, and the U.K. mean that it is available all year. It is well suited to succulent winter salads, when the selection of lettuce in supermarkets is generally less varied. Chinese cabbage is also good in stews, and it adds a crunchy texture to stir-fries.

CHINESE CELERY

Unlike the Western variety, Chinese celery stalks are thin, hollow, and very crisp, and range from pure white to dark green. Used as both a herb and a vegetable, Chinese celery is often stir-fried or used in soups and braised dishes.

CHINESE KALE

This green vegetable is popular in Thai cuisine. It has an almost earthy, slightly bitter taste and is usually served blanched and accompanied by oyster sauce. When buying, look for firm stems and fresh, dark-green leaves. Store in the bottom drawer of the refrigerator for up to four days.

CHINESE KEYS

Despite its name, this root vegetable is often used in Thai cuisine and rarely in Chinese. It is a member of the ginger family, with an aromatic sweet flavor that goes well in Thai curries.

CHINESE MUSTARD CABBAGE

These mustard plants are similar in appearance to cabbage. The whole leaf is eaten, usually shredded into soups and stir-fries. They add a fresh, astringent flavor.

CILANTRO

Fresh cilantro is the most popular fresh herb used in Thai cooking. It has a pungent, slightly citrus flavor. Leaves, stems, and roots are all used, so buy in big, fresh bunches if possible.

DURIAN

This large, spiky-skinned tropical fruit has such an unpleasantly strong aroma that it is banned from public transportation and hotels in Bangkok. It is expensive to buy a whole fruit, but you can sometimes buy frozen packs of skinless pieces of fruit.

EGGPLANT

Chinese eggplants are thinner with a more delicate flavor than the Mediterranean variety. They are used in many savory dishes, and in Thailand, some varieties are eaten raw served with a dip or sauce.

GALANGAL

This is a rhizome called laos or ka in Thailand. It is similar to ginger, but the skin is a pinkish color, and the flavor is more complex and mellow. Peel it thinly, and slice or grate the flesh. When sliced, it can be kept in an airtight container in the refrigerator for up to two weeks. If unavailable, ginger is an acceptable substitute.

GARLIC

This popular seasoning flavors almost all Thai, and many Chinese, dishes. In Thailand, garlic heads are smaller and thinner skinned, so they are often used whole, as well as finely chopped or crushed. Choose firm garlic, preferably with a pinkish tinge, and store in a cool, dry place, but not in the refrigerator.

GINGER

Ginger has a pungent, spicy, fresh taste. Fresh root is usually peeled, then finely chopped or grated—vary the amount of ginger used to suit your own taste. For just a hint, slice thickly and add to the dish when cooking, then remove just before serving. Fresh ginger is infinitely preferable to the powdered variety, which loses its flavor rapidly. Ginger should feel firm when you buy it. If you have more than you need, it can be used within a week. Store it in the freezer, as it can be grated from frozen.

KAFFIR LIME LEAVES

These come from the kaffir lime tree and are highly sought after for Thai cooking. They add a distinctive citrus flavor to curries, soups, and sauces. Buy them from larger supermarkets and Asian grocery stores, and keep them in a sealed plastic bag in the freezer. Lime zest can be used as an alternative.

KRACHAI

Also known as "lesser ginger," this is smaller and more spicy than either ginger or galangal. It can be bought fresh in Asian food stores, or dried in small packages.

LEMONGRASS

These look a bit like scallions, but are much tougher. The stems should be bashed to release the lemony flavor during cooking, then removed before serving. Alternatively, peel away the outer layers and chop the heart very finely.

LOTUS ROOT

This is the underwater rhizome of the lotus flower. It has a lacy appearance when sliced and a sweet, crunchy flavor. Fresh lotus root takes about two hours to cook, so consider using canned lotus root instead.

MOOLI

Also known as daikon or white radish, these look like smooth, white parsnips. They have a peppery, fresh taste and are often used in salads, peeled and thinly sliced or grated.

MUSHROOMS

Oyster mushrooms, with their subtle flavor and delicate, almost slippery texture, often feature in Chinese cooking. Shiitake mushrooms were originally grown only in Asia, but they are now grown all over the world. They are more often used dried in Chinese cooking, but may also be used fresh—the caps have a strong flavor and are generally sliced; the stalks are discarded. Cook the mushrooms gently for a short time, as they may toughen if overcooked.

PAPAYA

The unripe green flesh of this tropical fruit is often used in Thai cooking. It is not to be confused with a papaw, as both fruits are sometimes referred to as a paw paw. The papaya fruit can be as large as 22 pounds, but it is more common to find papayas that weigh just under a pound. Papayas ripen to a deep-orange color, and are delicious sliced and served as a dessert. Unripe papayas can be stuffed and either cooked or baked. In Thailand, papayas are abundant and are often served in green salad with lime juice and chilies. The seeds are usually discarded, but they are edible and have a very peppery flavor—ideal in a salad dressing. Place an almost ripe papaya in a paper bag so that it will ripen quickly at room temperature. Once fully ripe, it is best to keep the fruit in the refrigerator and eat as soon as possible. Papayas are a very good source of vitamins A and C, and the juice, or nectar, can be used as a meat tenderizer.

SCALLIONS

Long, slender scallions are the immature bulbs of yellow onions. They are frequently used in stir-fries, as they cook within minutes.

SHALLOTS

Small, mild-flavored members of the onion family, shallots have coppery-colored skins. Use them in the same way as onions, or thinly slice and deep-fry to use as a garnish.

SNOW PEAS

These tender pea pods with barely formed peas have a deliciously crisp texture. To prepare them for cooking, simply cut off the top and bottom, pulling away any string from the edges.

TAMARIND

This adds an essential sour taste to many dishes. It is extracted from the pods as a sticky brown pulp, which is soaked to make tamarind water.

TOFU

Tofu, or bean curd, has been used as an ingredient in Thai and Chinese cooking for over 1,000 years. Made from yellow soybeans that are soaked, ground, and briefly cooked, tofu is very rich in protein and low in calories. Because of its bland taste, it is ideally cooked with stronger flavorings. It is usually available in two types: a soft variety known as silken tofu that can be used for soups and desserts, and a firm, solid white block, which can be cubed or sliced, and included in stir-frying and braising. When using, cut into the required size with care, and do not stir too much when cooking; it simply needs to be heated through.

WATER CHESTNUTS

These are bulbs of an Asian water plant that look like and are a similar size to chestnuts. When peeled, the inner flesh is very crisp. Some Asian grocers sell them fresh, although canned, either whole or sliced, are almost as good.

WATER SPINACH

This is widely grown throughout Asia and is unrelated to ordinary spinach. The leaves are elongated and tender, and the stems fine and delicate. Water spinach requires minimal cooking. It is cooked in the same way as spinach, either steamed, stir-fried, or added to soups.

YARD-LONG BEANS

Although unrelated to green beans, they are similar in appearance, but about four times longer. As they grow, they start to curl and are often sold in looped bunches. Two varieties exist: a pale-green type and a much darker, thinner variety. They are very popular and may be found in great quantities in Chinese markets. The Cantonese often cook them with black beans or fermented bean curd, and in szechuan cooking, they are deep-fried. Store in the refrigerator for up to four days. To prepare, cut into lengths and use in exactly the same way as green beans.

DRY, CANNED, AND PRESERVED INGREDIENTS

BIRD'S NEST

 This is literally a bird's nest made from the spittle of a swallow and can occasionally be found in Chinese food stores. It is sold as a crunchy jelly that is often added to sauces, soups, and extravagant stuffings, and is an acquired taste. Since it is dried, it can be stored in a dry place for several years. To use, it should be soaked overnight in cold water, then simmered for 20 minutes in fresh water.

CASHEWS

 These milky-flavored nuts with a crunchy texture are often used whole or chopped in Chinese cooking, particularly as an ingredient in chicken dishes.

CASSIA

This is the bark taken from a cassia or laurel tree and is dark brown and flat in shape. It is similar to but slightly less subtle than cinnamon.

CHILIES

Dried red chilies are used throughout Thailand and in many regions of China. The drying process concentrates the flavor, making them more fiery. Look for dried chilies with a bright red color and a pungent aroma. If stored in a sealed container, they will keep almost indefinitely. Chili oil is made from crushed dried chilies or whole fresh chilies, and is used as both a seasoning and a dipping condiment. Chili powder is made from dried red chilies and is usually mixed with other spices and seasonings, ranging from mild and aromatic to very hot—always check the jar before using. Chili bean sauce is a thick, dark paste made from soybeans, chilies, and other spicy seasonings, and is very hot. Seal the jar after use and store in the refrigerator.

COCONUT MILK

 Rich, creamy coconut milk is extracted from the white flesh of the nut. It can be bought in cans or made by adding boiling water to a packet of coconut milk powder. Sometimes an opaque, white cream rises to the top of canned coconut milk and solidifies. You should shake the can before opening. If the milk is stored in an airtight container in the refrigerator, it will last for up to three days. However, it does not freeze well. Occasionally, freshly made coconut milk may be bought from Asian groceries. It is often used in Thai cooking, especially in curries, and may also be used in desserts.

CORIANDER

 Ground coriander is made from coriander seeds and has an almost sweet, spicy, fresh flavor. You can buy it already ground or, instead, toast whole seeds in the oven and grind them.

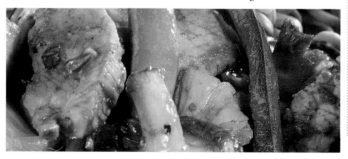

CREAMED COCONUT

 Made from coconut oils and other fats, this comes in a hard, white block. It is not a substitute for coconut milk and is usually added at the end of cooking to thicken a sauce or to add coconut flavor to a finished dish.

PEANUT OIL

 This oil has a mild, nutty flavor. Because it can be heated to high temperatures, it is ideal for both stir-frying and deep-frying.

HOISIN SAUCE

 This is a thick, dark, brownish-red sauce that is sweet, tangy, and spicy. Made from soybeans, salt, flour, sugar, vinegar, chili, garlic, and sesame oil, it may be used as a dip, in "red-cooking," and as a baste for roasted meats.

MUSHROOMS

 Many sorts of dried mushrooms are used in Thai and Chinese cooking. Cloud ear (black fungus) mushrooms need soaking in warm water for about twenty minutes before use. They have a subtle, mild flavor, and are highly regarded for their color and gelatinous flavor. Dried shiitake mushrooms have a very strong flavor and are used in small quantities. After soaking, the hard stalks are usually discarded or added to stock.

NAM PLA FISH SAUCE

 This is a golden-brown, thin sauce with a salty flavor and is made from salted and fermented fresh fish, usually anchovies. It is used in Thai cooking in much the same way as soy sauce is used in Chinese cooking. The fishy aroma is almost unpleasant when the bottle is opened, but this mellows when mixed with other ingredients, adding a unique Thai flavor.

NOODLES

There are many types of noodles used in Thai and Chinese cuisine. Cellophane noodles, also known as "glass noodles," are white and become transparent when cooked. Made from ground mung beans, they are never served on their own, but are added to soups or are deep-fried and used as a garnish. Egg noodles can be bought fresh, but the dried ones, which come in fine and medium, are just as good. Generally, flat noodles are used in soups, and round ones for stir-fries. Rice noodles are fine, opaque noodles made from rice flour, and are also called "rice sticks." These are common in southern China, the rice growing area of the country. Wheat is the primary grain in northern China and is made into noodles without egg. These noodles are sold in compressed square packages and bundles. Yifu noodles are round, yellow noodles, woven in a round cake and are often sold precooked.

OYSTER SAUCE

 This is a thick, brown sauce made from oysters cooked in soy sauce. It has a wonderfully rich, but not fishy, flavor, as this disappears during processing. Often used as a condiment, it is one of the most frequently used ingredients in southern Chinese cuisine.

PLUM SAUCE

s the name suggests, plum sauce is made from plums that are simmered with vinegar, sugar, ginger, chili, and other spices.

RICE

lutinous rice is a short-grain variety often used in desserts. It is sometimes referred to as "sticky rice." Thai jasmine rice is a long-grain rice with an aromatic and subtle flavor.

RICE PAPER WRAPPERS

his is made from a mixture of rice flour, water, and salt, which is rolled out by machine until it is paper-thin and dried. It comes in round or triangular pieces—which can be softened by placing between two damp dishtowels—and are used to make spring rolls.

RICE VINEGARS

here are several varieties: white vinegar is clear and mild; red vinegar is slightly sweet and quite salty, and is often used as a dipping sauce; black vinegar is very rich, yet mild; and sweet vinegar is very thick and dark-colored, and is flavored with star anise.

RICE WINE

ften used in Chinese cooking in both marinades and sauces, rice wine is made from glutinous rice and has a rich, mellow taste. Do not confuse rice wine with sake, the Japanese version, as it is very different. Pale dry sherry is a good substitute for rice wine.

SESAME OIL

his is a thick, dark-golden to brown, aromatic oil that is made from sesame seeds. It is rarely used in frying, as it has a low smoke-point, but when it is, it should be combined with another oil. It is often added to a finished dish in small quantities.

SESAME PASTE

esame paste is a rich, very creamy, brown paste made from sesame seeds. It is not the same as tahini paste from the Middle East. If unavailable, use smooth peanut butter, which has a similar texture.

SESAME SEEDS

hese are the dried seeds of the sesame herb. Unhulled, the seeds may be dull white to black in color, but once the hull is removed, the seeds are a creamy-white color. Sesame seeds are often used as a garnish or as a light coating to add crunch to food. Intensify their flavor by shaking over the heat in a frying pan until the seeds are lightly browned.

SHRIMP PASTE

ade from puréed, fermented, salted shrimp, this paste is popular in Thai cooking and adds a distinctive fishy flavor. There is also a Chinese version, which has an even stronger aroma. Use both sparingly. Dried salted shrimps are also available, which are sometimes used as a seasoning in stir-fries. They should be first soaked in warm water, then puréed in a blender, or made into a paste with a mortar and pestle.

SOY SAUCE

oth light and dark soy sauce feature frequently in Chinese and Thai cooking. It is made from a mixture of soybeans, flour, and water that are fermented together and allowed to age. The resulting liquid is distilled to make soy sauce. Light soy sauce has a lighter color and is more salty than the dark variety. It is often labeled as

"superior soy." Dark soy sauce is aged longer, and the color is almost black. Its flavor is stronger, and it is slightly thicker than light soy sauce. Confusingly, dark soy sauce is labeled in Thai and Chinese food shops as "soy superior sauce." It is also possible to buy a mushroom soy sauce, which is made by infusing dry straw mushrooms in a shrimp-flavored soy sauce.

STAR ANISE

his is an eight-pointed, star-shaped pod with a strong aniseed flavor. It is added whole to many Chinese dishes, but is usually removed before serving. It is also an important ingredient in Chinese five spice powder.

SUGAR

dded in small quantities to many savory Thai dishes, sugar balances the flavor of a dish and gives a shiny appearance to the sauces. Thai palm sugar comes in large lumps or slabs, which need to be broken into smaller pieces with a mallet. Brown coffee grounds make a good alternative.

SZECHUAN PEPPERCORNS

his small reddish spice has a distinct, woody flavor, and is more fragrantly spicy than hot. It is one of the spices in Chinese five spice powder. Also known as fargara and "Chinese pepper," Szechuan peppercorns are used extensively in Szechuan cooking. Unrelated to peppers, they are the dried berries of a shrub and have a slight numbing effect on the tongue.

THAI CURRY PASTE

ed curry paste is a strongly flavored spicy paste made mainly from dried red chilies, which are blended with other spices and herbs. There is also green curry paste, which is hotter and made from fresh green chilies.

THOUSAND-YEAR-OLD EGGS

resh duck eggs are often preserved in brine, which seeps into the shell, making the whites salty, and the yolks firm and orange colored. Thousand-year-old eggs are preserved in a mixture of clay, fine ash, and salt. The whites of the eggs turn a translucent black, and the yolks a grey-green color after a year or so. Unopened eggs can be kept for many months.

TURMERIC

his mild-flavored spice has a bitter, pungent flavor and adds a bright yellow hue to foods. Although it can sometimes be bought fresh, it is most often used in its dried, powdered form. Turmeric is widely available in supermarkets, and as with all spices, it should be stored in a cool, dark place for up to six months. It is nearly always an ingredient in curries.

YELLOW BEAN SAUCE

his thick, aromatic sauce is made with fermented yellow beans, flour, and salt, and adds a distinctive flavor to sauces.

EQUIPMENT

There is little equipment that is absolutely essential to preparing and cooking Thai and Chinese food, but many tools will make the task easier and give more authentic results.

BAMBOO STRAINER This is a wide, flat metal strainer with a bamboo handle. It makes removing cooked food from hot oil or water much easier. Of course, an ordinary metal slotted spoon may be used instead.

CHOPSTICKS Food is usually eaten with chopsticks in China, but in Thailand, a spoon and fork are more commonly used. Wooden chopsticks are inexpensive, but plastic ones are more hygienic and can be reused many times.

CLEAVERS These are used to slice, chop, shred, fillet, dice, and crush. It is such an all-purpose tool that skilled Thai and Chinese cooks need no other knives. These come in different weights: light, medium, and heavy. The best quality are made with tempered carbon steel, so that the blade can be kept razor sharp, although a good-quality, stainless-steel one is less likely to rust.

ELECTRIC RICE COOKER Since many meals are accompanied by rice, most modern Thai and Chinese kitchens have an electric rice cooker. It is the easiest way to cook rice to perfection with little attention.

SPATULA A long-handled spatula with a shovel-shaped end for stir-frying food is relatively inexpensive, although you can use a long-handled wooden spoon if you prefer.

STEAMERS You can either use a stainless-steel steamer with small, round perforations, which fits over a saucepan, or buy a more traditional bamboo steamer. You will need one or more tiers, plus a lid. It is a good idea to wash the bamboo steamer before using it for the first time and to steam it while empty for a few minutes.

WOK This is probably the most useful and versatile piece of equipment, and is used for stir-frying, deep-frying, and steaming. The traditional shape has deep, sloping sides and a rounded base to ensure quick, even cooking. In stir-frying, it is possible to move the food around without pieces spilling over the edges, and in deep-frying, the rounded shape means that considerably less oil is needed than in a conventional pan. This shape is, however, only suitable for use on a gas burner, and if yours is electric, you will need a wok with a flatter base that is specifically designed for such burners.

There are two basic types of wok: the Cantonese version, which has small handles on either side and may be wooden or metal, and the pau or Peking wok, which has a long handle. When choosing a wok, make sure it is large enough for your needs; most are about 12–14 inches in diameter, but some are much smaller. Even if you only cook for one or two people, a large wok is still preferable. Pick a heavier wok, but remember you will need to be able to lift it when full of food. Those made of carbon steel can take very high heat without scorching the food. Nonstick versions are now available, which means that you can reduce the fat in many recipes. Nonstick woks are also useful when adding ingredients with a high acid level, such as vinegar.

Wok accessories include domed lids, metal racks, and metal frames. Domed lids are usually made from light aluminum and are necessary for steaming and keeping food hot. A metal rack can easily be clipped on to the edge of the wok, making it useful for draining food. You will also need a wok stand—a metal frame that holds the wok firm and sufficiently far enough away from the heat. For safety, always make sure this is securely in place before setting your wok on it and starting to cook.

Before use, all woks, unless nonstick, should be seasoned. First, wash the wok in very hot, soapy water. This will remove the protective coat of oil applied by the manufacturer to prevent the wok from being marked by the packaging or damaged during transit. Pour 1 tablespoon of peanut or corn oil into the wok and rub it all over the inside with paper towels. Gently heat the wok for about 5 minutes, then wipe it clean. If the paper towel is black, you should repeat this process. With age, your wok will darken; this is normal and you should not scour it to remove this coloring. Always make sure that you dry the wok thoroughly before putting it away to keep it from rusting.

COOKING TECHNIQUES

DEEP-FRYING When deep-frying in a wok, pour in enough oil to come no more than one-third up the side. Gently heat until the required temperature is reached, preferably using a cooking thermometer. Alternatively, you can test the temperature by dropping in a small cube of bread; bubbles should quickly form all over the surface. Carefully add the food to the oil with tongs or a slotted spoon and move it around occasionally while cooking to keep the pieces separate. It is far better to cook in batches than to add all the food at once, as the oil may bubble up too much, and the temperature of the oil may drop, making the outside of the food soggy. Remove the food when cooked, and drain on paper towels to soak up any excess oil before serving. Always make sure that the wok is secure before you start cooking and never leave it unattended. A deep-fat fryer is a costly, but useful, piece of equipment if you deep-fry foods often, and you may find it is safer and easier to use than a wok.

STEAMING This is a gentle and moist method of cooking, especially good for delicate foods such as fish. It relies on the heat circulating around the food, so make sure you leave a little space between each item in the steamer. After arranging, place the steamer above simmering water in a wok or saucepan. To prevent food from sticking to the steamer, you can line it first with a cheesecloth. If desired, add a few slices of ginger and a bay leaf to the water. This not only adds a slight flavor to the food, but makes a wonderful aroma in the kitchen and can help mask cooking smells, especially if you are steaming fish. Steam for the recommended time, checking the water level in the pan or wok occasionally and adding more boiling water if necessary. If you do not have a steamer, you can use a wok instead. Place a rack or trivet in the wok, and pour in enough boiling water to come to just below the level of the trivet. Place the food to be steamed on a heatproof plate and put on top of the trivet. Cover and steam as before.

STIR-FRYING This quick-cook technique retains the fresh flavor, color, and texture of food. It is essential to have all ingredients prepared before you start cooking. Heat the wok for about a minute over a high heat, then add the oil and swirl it around to coat the bottom and about halfway up the sides. Continue heating until hot, but not smoking, so that the food starts to cook right away when added. Add the ingredients, one at a time, tossing and stirring continuously. Aromatics, such as garlic and ginger, are usually added first, followed by the main ingredients that need longer cooking, such as meat, and, finally, those that need little cooking, or only a brief heating through. Liquids and sauces are usually added towards the end of cooking, and then boiled for a minute or two.

SPICE MIXTURES AND FLAVORINGS Your finished dishes will have an unmistakable fresh flavor if you make your own basic seasoning mixtures, although they can be bought. Adjust the spices to taste.

CRISPY BASIL This makes an attractive garnish sprinkled over savory dishes. Use Thai basil if you can find it, although sweet Italian basil works just as well. Take 1 cup fresh basil leaves and 1 deseeded and finely sliced red chili. Heat 3 tablespoons of peanut oil in a wok until very hot, add the basil and chili, and stir-fry for 1–2 minutes or until crispy. Remove with a slotted spoon and drain on paper towels.

CRISPY SEAWEED This is often used as a garnish on Chinese dishes. Finely shred a piece of dark-green cabbage—savoy is ideal—and deep-fry in peanut oil at 350° F for about 1 minute until crispy. Sprinkle with a little finely ground sea salt and sprinkle over the dish, or serve separately as a side dish.

FRESH COCONUT MILK Take a fresh coconut, push a large skewer into the three holes at the top, and drain out the liquid. Put the coconut in a thick plastic bag and hit it hard with a hammer to break the shell. Remove the outer shell from the flesh with a sharp knife, then peel away the thin brown skin. Shred the flesh, put in a food processor, and blend until very fine. Pour in 1¼ cups of boiling water, briefly process, then leave for 15 minutes. Strain the mixture through a sieve lined with cheesecloth. When drained, draw the corners of the cheesecloth together, and squeeze out the last drops of liquid. Repeat the process with the coconut and an additional 1¼ cups of boiling water, and add to the first batch of coconut milk. Store in the refrigerator for up to 48 hours, but do not freeze. A solid, fatty cream may rise to the top, so stir the liquid well before using.

You can also make coconut milk from dried coconut. Put 4 cups in a saucepan with 1¼ cups of water, and simmer for 3–4 minutes. Briefly blend in a food processor, then make in the same way as fresh coconut milk, adding a second batch of boiling water to the squeezed-dry coconut.

GREEN CURRY PASTE Roughly chop 6 scallions, 1 lemongrass stalk, 2 peeled garlic cloves, 8 fresh green chilies (remove the seeds if you want a milder paste), a 1-inch piece of ginger, and 1 cup cilantro stalks and roots. Remove and discard the central vein from 2 kaffir lime leaves, and finely shred. Put all the ingredients in a food processor with 2 tablespoons of peanut oil and a pinch of salt. Blend to a paste, then transfer to a jar, and store for up to three weeks in the refrigerator.

RED CURRY PASTE Remove the seeds from 8 fresh red chilies and roughly chop. Put in a food processor with a 1-inch piece of ginger, 2 peeled shallots, 1 lemongrass stalk, and 4 peeled garlic cloves, all roughly chopped. Add 2 teaspoons of coriander seeds, 1 teaspoon of cumin seeds, 1 teaspoon of hot paprika, a pinch each of turmeric and salt, 1 tablespoon of lime juice, and 2 tablespoons of peanut oil. Blend to a paste, transfer to a jar, and store for up to three weeks in the refrigerator.

CUSTOMS AND TRADITIONS

C hinese and Thai food has become increasingly popular during recent years. There are many similarities between the two cuisines, yet their history, climate, and culture has created subtle differences between them.

CHINESE CUISINE

A lthough China is a vast country, the basic principles of cooking is remarkably similar throughout the regions. Economical, fuel-saving methods of cooking have developed over the years, such as fast and furious stir-frying, where food is cut up into small, even-sized pieces so it cooks in very little time; steaming, where baskets are stacked layer upon layer; and slow simmering in a large pot to make use of the last remaining embers of the fire. Few things go to waste in the Chinese kitchen, and some of their greatest delicacies have been created from scraps that Westerners would simply throw away.

Chinese cuisine falls into four main culinary regions: Cantonese or southern, Peking or northern, North China, and Shanghai or eastern. Peking cuisine is famous for seafood, pork, and sweet-and-sour dishes, as well as more unusual ingredients, like bird's nest and shark's fin. In Chinese, the word fan means both rice and meal, and rice accompanies almost every meal in the south. Long-grain rice is the most commonly used, but Thai jasmine rice is served on special occasions, as is sticky or glutinous rice, which is also used for desserts.

Peking or northern cuisine is associated with a refined style of cooking, since many classical dishes have been handed down from the imperial kitchen. Here, there is a notable use of lamb, garlic, scallions, and leeks. Food tends to be sweet and sour, but with much more emphasis on the sour rather than sweet. North China is an area where wheat, rather than rice, is grown, and wheat-based noodles are popular. In Shanghai or eastern China, vegetables and rice are plentiful, and it is here that rice wine and vinegar are made. Many dishes from this region have a sweet flavor, as sugar is commonly used as a seasoning. Szechuan cuisine is very fiery and spicy, and chilies and Szechuan pepper feature in virtually every savory dish.

THE CHINESE MEAL

In China, dishes are served all together, not in separate courses. The Chinese rarely eat on their own and enjoy sharing a meal, dining with family or a group of friends. Rice is served in individual dishes, topped with a portion from a central meat or vegetable dish. When this has been eaten, each person takes some of another dish using chopsticks (which should never touch the lips).

Many dishes have descriptive and romantic names, such as "five flower pork" for belly pork, named after the five layers of skin, fat, and lean. Certain numbers are considered lucky, so

dishes are often given names, such as "eight treasures," even though there may not be eight ingredients! Phoenix and dragon are the terms sometimes used for shrimp and chicken.

In Szechuan, chilies, fermented bean paste, and sesame oil are used in varying combinations to produce dishes with evocative names, including "strange taste" (guai wei), "familiar taste" (jiachanh wei), and "peppery taste" (xiangla wei). Drinks are not usually taken with the meal, but a bowl of soup is often provided to wash the food down when needed. At the end of the meal, tea may be served. Grown in China for more than 3,000 years, teas come in many varieties, and can be divided into three main types: green tea, oolong tea, and black tea. Green tea is unfermented and is a pale, fragrant drink served without milk or sugar. Gunpowder, one of the green teas, was so named by the British because the tea resembled lead shot. Jasmine, another green tea, is flavored with dried jasmine petals. Oolong tea is semifermented with a stronger flavor, but it is not as strong as black tea, which is fully fermented and has a hint of sweetness. Black teas include keemum, which has a slightly nutty flavor, and lapsang souchong.

Although the Chinese people have an incredibly sweet tooth and enjoy desserts and cakes, these are not served at the end of the meal, as in the West. Instead, they are eaten at formal banquets, where they are served partway through the meal.

CELEBRATIONS

Chinese New Year is probably the best-known celebration and is a time of reunion and thanksgiving. It is a religious ceremony in honor of Heaven and Earth, the gods of the household, and family ancestors. The head of each household offers incense, flowers, food, and wine to ensure good fortune in the coming year. On New Year's Eve a banquet called weilu, meaning "surrounding the stove," is held, celebrating both present and past generations. Every dish served has a name that symbolizes either honor, health, or wealth. A soup, for example, may be called "broth of prosperity," and strands of vermicelli referred to as "silvery threads of longevity."

After the feast, parents give their children small, red envelopes that contain "lucky" money. In the next few days, friends and relatives visit, and more meals must be prepared. Snacks and sweetmeats, such as pomegranate seeds, candied lotus root, and almonds—all representing fertility and long life—are offered before the main dishes.

At the heart of many Chinese celebrations are the principles of balance and harmony. The beginning of each new season is important, as are the Buddhist and Taoist principles of yin and yang (female and male). Cooking ingredients are mixed and matched in the same way; sweet and sour or hot and sour, for example. On birthdays, noodles are usually served to represent long life. For luck, they should always be eaten whole, not broken into pieces. Dim sum, meaning "heart's delight," are popular Chinese snacks. These dumplings are filled with either vegetables or spiced meat, and are often deep-fried or steamed. They are traditionally eaten with tea for breakfast or lunch, or sold on the street to be eaten between meals. They play an important part during most festivals, including Chinese New Year, when they are eaten in place of normal meals.

THAI CUISINE

T hai food has been influenced by many countries, notably India, Burma, and especially China. Yet, the Thais have refined these to a unique cuisine of their own, characterized by the contrasting flavors of sharp citrus lime leaves and lemongrass, hot chilies, ginger and galangal, and sour tamarind, often brought together and mellowed by creamy coconut milk. Thai cuisine is similar to Chinese in that rice is a staple food (the Thai words used when inviting guests are "come and have rice with us"), together with plenty of fresh vegetables and only small amounts of meat. Dairy products are used sparingly, and for both religious and climatic reasons, red meats, such as beef, feature in few dishes.

As in Chinese cooking, food has a subtle balance of sweet, sour, and salty. Fish has always been important in the Thai diet, as the entire country is crossed by rivers and the coastline stretches for miles. Freshwater fish and shellfish are plentiful. Flooded rice fields sustain ducks, frogs, eels, and fish. Much of this is dried, salted, or made into fermented sauces and pastes, which add a distinctive flavor to many dishes. Thailand is an extremely fertile land, with a tropical climate and cooler central highlands, where an abundance of different ingredients are found. The Thais produce some of the finest foods in the world, and this is the only country in Asia to export more food than it imports.

Thai people are passionate about food. Shopping for food is as much of a skill as cooking it. Street markets are very much a way of life; everything arrives fresh in the morning, and by mid-afternoon, almost everything has been sold.

THE THAI MEAL

A Thai meal is all about sharing. It generally consists of a number of different dishes, plus a huge bowl of rice. Sometimes there is a soup or a curry, some noodles, and fresh fruit, such as rambutans, mangosteens, and durians. All these dishes come to the table at the same time, so everyone has the chance to sample a little of each. Just as in China, a large pile of rice on individual plates will be topped with one or two portions from the dishes. When these are finished, other dishes will be tasted.

Food is eaten either with a spoon and fork or with fingers, although noodles are eaten with chopsticks. A knife is not needed, because all the food has been cut up before cooking. Desserts are served only on special occasions, and generally a meal will end with fruit.

In the recipes in this book, and when eating out in Thai restaurants, you may come across some of the following terms.

GAENG This is a curry that is often quite hot. Gaeng ped is a red curry, and gaeng phanaeng is a dry curry that has a thicker, milder sauce.

GAENG CHUD This is soup, and one of the best known varieties is tom yam kung, which is made with shrimp. Another popular soup is tom khaa gai, which is made with chicken, galangal, and coconut milk.

KHANOM This is a sweetened dish, although it may be a savory food, and often consists of small, individual items served in banana-leaf pockets.

MEE OR SEN These are noodles that may be made from rice, wheat, or mung beans. Kuiteow are large, fresh noodles and are usually fried with vegetables. Mee krob are wheat noodles that are deep-fried, coated with a sugar syrup, and served as a savory.

CELEBRATIONS

Most important occasions in Thailand have a religious element, and before the adaptation of the Christian Sunday, working days were broken up by holy days. April 6th is Chakri day, when the founding of the present dynasty is celebrated, and flowers are taken to the temple of the Emerald Buddha. The king's birthday, the anniversary of his coronation, and the queen's birthday are all national holidays, and are celebrated with parades and fireworks. Elaborate banquets have a great part to play in the celebrations, and presentation is very important, with food exquisitely garnished with carved fruit and vegetables. The two greatest events in any Thai person's life are when a son becomes a monk for a short time (as most Thai males do) and marriage, which is still regarded as the union of two families, rather than individuals. At weddings, the Thai sweet look choob is served—at one time, this was only eaten by kings. This is made from a soybean paste with sugar and coconut juice, and it is molded into tiny fruit and vegetable shapes. The importance of family is evident in the Thai approach to dining, whether at a home-cooked meal or in a posh restaurant.

CLEAR CHICKEN & MUSHROOM SOUP

INGREDIENTS   Serves 4

2 large chicken legs, about
   1 lb. total weight
1 tbsp. peanut oil
1 tsp. sesame oil
1 onion, peeled and very
   thinly sliced
1 in. piece ginger, peeled and
   very finely chopped
5 cups clear chicken stock
1 lemongrass stalk, bruised
⅓ cup long-grain rice

1 cup wiped and finely sliced
   button mushrooms
4 scallions, trimmed, cut into
   2-in. pieces, and shredded
1 tbsp. dark soy sauce
4 tbsp. dry sherry
salt and freshly ground black
   pepper

1 Skin the chicken legs and remove any fat. Cut each in half to make 2 thigh and 2 drumstick portions, and set aside. Heat the peanut and sesame oils in a large saucepan. Add the sliced onion and cook gently for 10 minutes or until soft but not beginning to brown.

2 Add the chopped ginger to the saucepan, and cook for about 30 seconds, stirring constantly to prevent it from sticking, then pour in the stock. Add the chicken and the lemongrass, cover, and simmer gently for 15 minutes. Stir in the rice and cook for an additional 15 minutes or until the chicken is cooked.

3 Remove the chicken from the saucepan and leave until cool enough to handle. Finely shred the flesh, then return to the saucepan with the mushrooms, scallions, soy sauce, and sherry. Simmer for 5 minutes or until the rice and mushrooms are tender. Remove the lemongrass.

4 Season the soup to taste with salt and pepper. Ladle into warmed serving bowls, making sure each has an equal amount of shredded chicken and vegetables, and serve immediately.

FOOD FACT

When using sesame oil for stir-frying, as in this recipe, it is important to use it with another cooking oil, like peanut or sunflower oil—otherwise it will burn.

CREAMY CHICKEN & TOFU SOUP

INGREDIENTS

Serves 4–6

½ lb. firm tofu, drained

3 tbsp. peanut oil

1 garlic clove, peeled and crushed

1-in. piece ginger, peeled and finely chopped

1-in. piece galangal, peeled and finely sliced (if available)

1 lemongrass stalk, bruised

¼ tsp. ground turmeric

3 cups chicken stock

2½ cups coconut milk

2 cups tiny cauliflower florets

1 medium carrot, peeled and thinly sliced

¾ cup trimmed and halved green beans

¼ lb. thin egg noodles

1 cup shredded cooked chicken

salt and freshly ground black pepper

1 Cut the tofu into ½-in. cubes, then pat dry on paper towels.

2 Heat 1 tablespoon of the oil in a nonstick skillet. Fry the tofu in 2 batches for 3–4 minutes or until golden brown. Remove, drain on paper towels, and set aside.

3 Heat the remaining oil in a large saucepan. Add the garlic, ginger, galangal, and lemongrass, and cook for about 30 seconds. Stir in the turmeric, then pour in the stock and coconut milk, and bring to a boil. Reduce the heat to a gentle simmer, add the cauliflower and carrots, and simmer for 10 minutes. Add the green beans and simmer for an additional 5 minutes.

4 Meanwhile, bring a large saucepan of lightly salted water to a boil. Add the noodles, turn off the heat, cover, and leave to cook, or cook according to the package instructions.

5 Remove the lemongrass from the soup. Drain the noodles and stir into the soup with the chicken and browned tofu. Season to taste with salt and pepper, then simmer gently for 2–3 minutes or until heated through. Serve immediately in warmed soup bowls.

FOOD FACT

Tofu is a white curd made from soybeans. It originated in China and is made in a similar way to cheese.

WONTON NOODLE SOUP

INGREDIENTS

Serves 4

4 dried shiitake mushrooms, wiped
¾ cup peeled and finely chopped raw shrimp
¼ lb. ground pork
4 water chestnuts, finely chopped
4 scallions, trimmed and finely sliced
1 medium egg white

salt and freshly ground black pepper
1½ tsp. cornstarch
1 package fresh wonton wrappers
5 cups chicken stock
¾-in. piece ginger, peeled and sliced
3 oz. thin egg noodles
1 cup shredded bok choy

1 Place the mushrooms in a bowl, cover with warm water, and let soak for 1 hour. Drain, remove, and discard the stalks, and finely chop the mushrooms. Return to the bowl with the shrimp, pork, water chestnuts, 2 of the scallions, and the egg white. Season to taste with salt and pepper. Mix well.

2 Mix the cornstarch with 1 tablespoon of cold water to make a paste. Place a wonton wrapper on a board, and brush the edges with the paste. Drop a little less than 1 teaspoon of the pork mixture in the center, then fold in half to make a triangle, pressing the edges together. Bring the 2 outer corners together, pressing together with a little more paste. Continue until all the pork mixture is used up; you should have 16–20 wontons.

3 Pour the stock into a large, wide saucepan, add the ginger slices, and bring to a boil. Add the wontons and simmer for about 5 minutes. Add the noodles and cook for 1 minute. Stir in the bok choy and cook for an additional 2 minutes or until the noodles and bok choy are tender, and the wontons have floated to the surface and are cooked through.

4 Ladle the soup into warmed bowls, discarding the ginger. Sprinkle with the remaining sliced scallions, and serve immediately.

FOOD FACT

Wonton wrappers are thin sheets, about 4 in. square, of noodle dough made from eggs and flour. Buy them fresh or frozen from larger supermarkets and Asian markets.

THAI SHELLFISH SOUP

INGREDIENTS   Serves 4–6

¾ lb. raw shrimp

¾ lb. firm white fish, such as
  monkfish

6 oz. small squid

1 tbsp. lime juice

1 lb. live mussels

2 cups coconut milk

1 tbsp. peanut oil

2 tbsp. Thai red curry paste

1 lemongrass stalk, bruised

3 kaffir lime leaves, finely
  shredded

2 tbsp. Thai fish sauce

salt and freshly ground black
  pepper

fresh cilantro, to garnish

1 Peel the shrimp. Using a sharp knife, remove the black vein along the back of the shrimp. Pat dry with paper towels and set aside.

2 Skin the fish, pat dry, and cut into 1-in. chunks. Place in a bowl with the shrimp and the squid. Sprinkle with the lime juice and set aside.

3 Scrub the mussels, removing their beards and any barnacles. Discard any mussels that are open, damaged, or do not close when tapped. Place in a large saucepan and add ⅔ cup of coconut milk.

4 Cover, bring to a boil, then simmer for 5 minutes or until the mussels open, shaking the saucepan occasionally. Lift out the mussels, discarding any unopened ones, strain the liquid through a cheesecloth-lined sieve, and set aside.

5 Rinse and dry the saucepan. Heat the peanut oil, add the curry paste, and cook for 1 minute, stirring all the time. Add the lemongrass, lime leaves, fish sauce, the strained mussel liquid, and the remaining coconut milk. Bring the contents of the saucepan to a very gentle simmer.

6 Add the fish mixture to the saucepan, and simmer for 2–3 minutes or until just cooked. Stir in the mussels, with or without their shells, as preferred. Season to taste with salt and pepper, then garnish with cilantro. Ladle into warmed bowls and serve immediately.

FOOD FACT

Squeezing lime juice on top of seafood improves its texture, as the acid in the juice firms up the flesh.

MU SHU PORK

INGREDIENTS   Serves 4

6 oz. pork fillet

2 tsp. Chinese rice wine or dry sherry

2 tbsp. light soy sauce

1 tsp. cornstarch

1 oz. dried tiger lily buds, soaked and drained

2 tbsp. peanut oil

3 medium eggs, lightly beaten

1 tsp. freshly grated ginger

3 scallions, trimmed and thinly sliced

⅔ cup bamboo shoots, in fine strips

salt and freshly ground black pepper

8 mandarin pancakes, steamed

hoisin sauce

sprigs of cilantro, to garnish

1 Cut the pork across the grain into ½-in. slices, then cut into thin strips. Place in a bowl with the Chinese rice wine or sherry, soy sauce, and cornstarch. Mix well and set aside. Trim off the tough ends of the dried tiger lily buds, then cut in half and set aside.

2 Heat a wok or skillet, and add 1 tablespoon of the peanut oil. When hot, add the eggs, and cook for 1 minute, stirring constantly until scrambled. Remove and set aside. Wipe the wok clean with paper towels.

3 Return the wok to the heat, add the remaining oil, and, when hot, transfer the pork strips from the marinade mixture to the wok, shaking off as much marinade as possible. Stir-fry for 30 seconds, then add the ginger, scallions, and bamboo shoots, and pour in the marinade. Stir-fry for 2–3 minutes.

4 Return the scrambled eggs to the wok, season to taste with salt and pepper, and stir for a few seconds until mixed well and heated through. Divide the mixture between the pancakes, drizzle each with 1 teaspoon of hoisin sauce, and roll up. Garnish and serve immediately.

HELPFUL HINT

Tiger lily buds, also known as "golden needles," are dried, unopened lily flowers. They are about 2 in. long, have a slightly furry texture, and are strongly fragrant. Buy those that are bright gold in color, and store in a cool, dark place. They need to be soaked in hot water for about 30 minutes before use, then rinsed and squeezed dry. Omit them if you prefer, and increase the quantity of pork to ½ lb.

CRISPY PORK WONTONS

INGREDIENTS

Serves 4

1 small onion, peeled and roughly chopped

2 garlic cloves, peeled and crushed

1 green chili, deseeded and chopped

1-in. piece ginger, peeled and roughly chopped

1 lb. lean ground pork

4 tbsp. freshly chopped cilantro

1 tsp. Chinese five spice powder

salt and freshly ground black pepper

20 wonton wrappers

1 medium egg, lightly beaten

vegetable oil for deep-frying

chili sauce, to serve

1 Place the onion, garlic, chili, and ginger in a food processor, and blend until very finely chopped. Add the pork, cilantro, and Chinese five spice powder. Season to taste with salt and pepper, then blend again briefly to mix. Divide the mixture into 20 equal portions and, with floured hands, shape each into a walnut-sized ball.

2 Brush the edges of a wonton wrapper with beaten egg, place a pork ball in the center, then bring the corners to the center and pinch together to make a pouch. Repeat with the remaining pork balls and wrappers.

3 Pour sufficient oil into a heavy-based saucepan or deep-fat fryer so that it is one-third full, and heat to 350° F. Deep-fry the wontons in 3 or 4 batches for 3–4 minutes, or until cooked through, golden, and crisp. Drain on paper towels. Serve the crispy pork wontons immediately, allowing 5 per person, with some chili sauce for dipping.

HELPFUL HINT

When frying the wontons, use a deep, heavy-based saucepan or deep-fat fryer fitted with a wire basket. Never fill the pan more than one-third full with oil, and heat over a moderate heat until it reaches the required temperature. Either use a cooking thermometer, or drop a cube of day-old bread into the hot oil. It will turn golden-brown in 45 seconds when the oil is hot enough.

MIXED SATAY STICKS

INGREDIENTS

Serves 4

12 jumbo raw shrimp
¾ lb. beef steak
1 tbsp. lemon juice
1 garlic clove, peeled and
  crushed
salt
2 tsp. dark brown sugar
1 tsp. ground cumin
1 tsp. ground coriander
¼ tsp. ground turmeric
1 tbsp. peanut oil
fresh cilantro, to garnish

**FOR THE SPICY PEANUT
  SAUCE:**
1 shallot, peeled and very
  finely chopped
1 tsp. raw sugar
¼ cup creamed coconut,
  chopped
pinch of chili powder
1 tbsp. dark soy sauce
½ cup crunchy peanut butter

1 Soak 8 bamboo skewers in cold water for at least 30 minutes. Peel the shrimp, leaving the tails on. Using a sharp knife, remove the black vein along the back of the shrimp. Cut the beef into ½-in.-wide strips. Place the shrimp and beef in separate bowls, and sprinkle each with ½ tablespoon of the lemon juice.

2 Mix together the garlic, sugar, cumin, coriander, turmeric, peanut oil, and a pinch of salt to make a paste. Lightly brush over the shrimp and beef. Cover, and place in the refrigerator to marinate for at least 30 minutes—longer if possible.

3 Meanwhile, make the sauce. Pour ½ cup of water into a small saucepan, add the shallot and sugar, and heat gently until

the sugar has dissolved. Stir in the creamed coconut and chili powder. When melted, remove from the heat and stir in the peanut butter. Let cool slightly, then spoon into a serving dish.

4 Thread 3 shrimp onto each of 4 skewers, and divide the sliced beef between the remaining skewers.

5 Cook the skewers under the preheated broiler for 4–5 minutes, turning occasionally. The shrimp should be opaque and pink, and the beef browned on the outside, but still pink in the center. Transfer to warmed individual serving plates, garnish with a few fresh cilantro leaves, and serve immediately with the warm peanut sauce.

CORN FRITTERS

INGREDIENTS   Serves 4

4 tbsp. peanut oil
1 small onion, peeled and
  finely chopped
1 red chili, deseeded and
  finely chopped
1 garlic clove, peeled and
  crushed
1 tsp. ground coriander
11 oz. corn

6 scallions, trimmed and finely
  sliced
1 medium egg, lightly beaten
salt and freshly ground black
  pepper
3 tbsp. all-purpose flour
1 tsp. baking powder
scallion curls, to garnish
Thai-style chutney, to serve

1 Heat 1 tablespoon of the peanut oil in a skillet, add the onion, and cook gently for 7–8 minutes or until beginning to soften. Add the chili, garlic, and ground coriander, and cook for 1 minute, stirring continuously. Remove from the heat.

2 Drain the corn and tip into a mixing bowl. Lightly crush with a potato masher to break down the corn a little. Add the cooked onion mixture to the bowl with the scallions and beaten egg. Season to taste with salt and pepper, then stir to mix together. Sift the flour and baking powder over the mixture and stir in.

3 Heat 2 tablespoons of the peanut oil in a large skillet. Drop 4 or 5 heaping teaspoonfuls of the corn mixture into the pan, and using a fish slice or spatula, flatten each to make a ½-in.-thick fritter.

4 Fry the fritters for 3 minutes or until golden brown on the underside, turn over, and fry for an additional 3 minutes or until cooked through and crisp.

5 Remove the fritters from the pan and drain on paper towels. Keep warm while cooking the remaining fritters, adding a little more oil if needed. Garnish the fritters with scallion curls, and serve immediately with a Thai-style chutney.

HELPFUL HINT

To make a scallion curl, trim off the root and the green top to leave a 4-in. piece. Make a 1¼-in. cut down from the top, then make another cut at a right angle to the first cut. Continue making fine cuts. Soak the scallions in iced water for about 20 minutes until they open up and curl.

THAI CRAB CAKES

INGREDIENTS   Serves 4

1 cup white and brown
   crabmeat
1 tsp. ground coriander
¼ tsp. chili powder
¼ tsp. ground turmeric
2 tsp. lime juice
1 tsp. light brown sugar
1-in. piece ginger, peeled and
   grated
3 tbsp. freshly chopped
   cilantro

2 tsp. finely chopped
   lemongrass
2 tbsp all-purpose flour
2 medium eggs, separated
1 cup fresh white bread
   crumbs
3 tbsp. peanut oil
lime wedges, to garnish
mixed lettuce leaves, to serve

1 Place the crabmeat in a bowl with the ground coriander, chili, turmeric, lime juice, sugar, ginger, chopped cilantro, lemongrass, flour, and egg yolks. Mix together well.

2 Divide the mixture into 12 equal portions and form each into a small patty about 2 in. across. Lightly whisk the egg whites and put into a dish. Place the bread crumbs on a separate plate.

3 Dip each crab cake in the egg whites, then in the bread crumbs, turning to coat both sides. Place on a plate, cover, and chill in the refrigerator until ready to cook.

4 Heat the oil in a large skillet. Add 6 crab cakes and cook for 3 minutes on each side or until crisp, golden brown on the outside, and cooked through.

Remove, drain on paper towels, and keep warm while cooking the remaining cakes. Arrange on plates, garnish with lime wedges, and serve immediately with lettuce leaves.

HELPFUL HINT

Prepare freshly steamed crabs as follows. Twist off the legs and claws, then crack them open and remove the meat. Turn the crab onto its back and twist off the bony, pointed flap. Place the tip of a knife between the main shell and the point where the legs were attached, twist the blade, lift up and remove the body, then scrape out the brown meat. Pull away and discard the soft, grey gills. Split the body in half, and using a skewer, remove the white meat from the cavities.

SESAME SHRIMP TOASTS

INGREDIENTS

Serves 4

¾ cup peeled, cooked shrimp
1 tbsp. cornstarch
2 scallions, peeled and
  roughly chopped
2 tsp. freshly grated ginger
2 tsp. dark soy sauce
pinch of Chinese five spice
  powder (optional)
1 small egg, beaten

salt and freshly ground black
  pepper
6 thin slices day-old white
  bread
3 tbsp. sesame seeds
vegetable oil for deep-frying
chili sauce, to serve

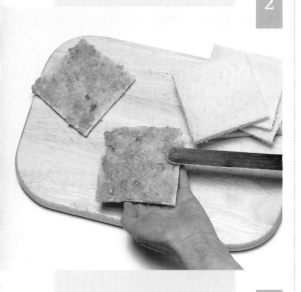

1 Place the shrimp in a food processor or blender with the cornstarch, scallions, ginger, soy sauce, and Chinese five spice powder. Blend to a fairly smooth paste. Spoon into a bowl and stir in the beaten egg. Season to taste with salt and pepper.

2 Cut the crusts off the bread. Spread the shrimp paste in an even layer on one side of each slice. Sprinkle over the sesame seeds, and press down lightly.

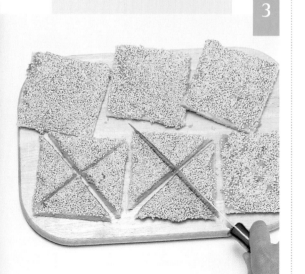

3 Cut each slice diagonally into 4 triangles. Place on a board and chill in the refrigerator for 30 minutes.

4 Pour enough oil into a heavy-based saucepan or deep-fat fryer so that it is one-third full. Heat until it reaches a temperature of 350° F. Cook the toast in batches of 5 or 6, carefully lowering them seeded-side down into the oil. Deep-fry for 2–3 minutes or until lightly browned, then turn over and cook for 1 more minute. Using a slotted spoon, lift out the pieces of toast, and drain on paper towels. Keep warm while frying the remaining pieces. Arrange on a warmed platter, and serve immediately with some chili sauce for dipping.

HELPFUL HINT

The toasts can be prepared to the end of Step 3 up to 12 hours in advance. Cover with plastic wrap and chill in the refrigerator until needed. It is important to use bread that is a day or two old, not fresh bread. Make sure that the shrimp are well-drained before puréeing— pat them dry on paper towels, if necessary.

SWEET-&-SOUR CRISPY FISH

INGREDIENTS   Serves 4–6

1 lb. white fish fillet, skinned
1½ cups all-purpose flour
salt and freshly ground black
    pepper
2 tbsp. cornstarch
2 tbsp. arrowroot
vegetable oil for deep-frying

**FOR THE SWEET-&-SOUR
SAUCE:**
4 tbsp. orange juice
2 tbsp. white wine vinegar
2 tbsp. dry sherry
1 tbsp. dark soy sauce
1 tbsp. golden brown sugar
2 tsp. tomato paste
1 red bell pepper, deseeded
    and diced
2 tsp. cornstarch

1 Cut the fish into 1 x 2-in. pieces. Place 4 tablespoons of the flour in a small bowl, season with salt and pepper to taste, then add the fish strips, a few at a time, tossing until coated.

2 Sift the remaining flour into a bowl with a pinch of salt, the cornstarch, and arrowroot. Gradually whisk in 2½ cups ice water to make a smooth, thin batter.

3 Heat the oil in a wok or deep-fat fryer to 375° F. Working in batches, dip the fish strips in the batter, and deep-fry them for 3–5 minutes or until crisp. Using a slotted spoon, remove the strips, and drain on paper towels.

4 Meanwhile, make the sauce. Place 3 tablespoons of the orange juice, the vinegar, sherry, soy sauce, sugar, tomato paste, and red bell pepper in a small saucepan. Bring to a boil, lower the heat, and simmer for 3 minutes.

5 Blend the cornstarch with the remaining orange juice, stir into the sauce, and simmer, stirring, for 1 minute or until thickened. Arrange the fish on a warmed platter or individual plates. Drizzle with a little of the sauce, and serve immediately with the remaining sauce.

TASTY TIP

Any firm white fish can be used for this dish, as long as it is fairly thick. Your fish retailer can tell you which varieties are suitable.

SPICY BEEF PANCAKES

INGREDIENTS
Serves 4

½ cup all-purpose flour
pinch of salt
½ tsp. Chinese five spice
  powder
1 large egg yolk
⅔ cup milk
4 tsp. sunflower oil
slices of scallion, to garnish

FOR THE SPICY BEEF FILLING:
1 tbsp. sesame oil
4 scallions, sliced

½-in. piece ginger, peeled and
  finely shredded
1 garlic clove, peeled and
  crushed
¾ lb. sirloin steak, trimmed
  and cut into strips
1 red chili, deseeded and
  finely chopped
1 tsp. sherry vinegar
1 tsp. dark brown sugar
1 tbsp. dark soy sauce

1 Sift the flour, salt, and Chinese five spice powder into a bowl, and make a well in the center. Add the egg yolk and a little of the milk. Gradually beat in, drawing in the flour to make a smooth batter. Whisk in the rest of the milk.

2 Heat 1 teaspoon of the sunflower oil in a small, heavy-based skillet. Pour in just enough batter to thinly coat the base of the pan. Cook over a medium heat for 1 minute or until the underside of the pancake is golden brown.

3 Turn or toss the pancake, and cook for 1 minute or until the other side of the pancake is golden brown. Make 7 more pancakes with the remaining batter. Stack them on a warmed plate as you make them, with greaseproof paper between each pancake. Cover with aluminum foil and keep warm in a low oven.

4 Make the filling. Heat a wok or large frying pan, add the sesame oil, and when hot, add the scallions, ginger, and garlic, and stir-fry for 1 minute. Add the beef strips, stir-fry for 3–4 minutes, then stir in the chili, vinegar, sugar, and soy sauce. Cook for 1 minute, then remove from the heat.

5 Spoon one eighth of the filling over one half of each pancake. Fold the pancakes in half, then fold in half again. Garnish the pancakes with a few slices of scallion and serve immediately.

LION'S HEAD PORK BALLS

INGREDIENTS   Serves 4

½ cup glutinous rice
1 lb. lean ground pork
2 garlic cloves, peeled and
  crushed
1 tbsp. cornstarch
½ tsp. Chinese five spice
  powder
2 tsp. dark soy sauce
1 tbsp. Chinese rice wine or
  dry sherry
2 tbsp. freshly chopped cilantro
salt and freshly ground black
  pepper

**FOR THE SWEET CHILI
DIPPING SAUCE:**
2 tsp. superfine sugar
1 tbsp. sherry vinegar
1 tbsp. light soy sauce
1 shallot, peeled and very
  finely chopped
1 small red chili, deseeded
  and finely chopped
2 tsp. sesame oil

1 Place the rice in a bowl, and pour in plenty of cold water. Cover and soak for 2 hours. Tip into a sieve and drain well.

2 Place the pork, garlic, cornstarch, Chinese five spice powder, soy sauce, Chinese rice wine or sherry, and cilantro in a bowl. Season to taste with salt and pepper, and mix together.

3 With slightly wet hands, shape the pork mixture into 20 walnut-sized balls, then roll in the rice to coat. Place the balls slightly apart in a steamer or a colander set over a saucepan of boiling water, cover, and steam for 20 minutes or until cooked through.

4 Meanwhile, make the dipping sauce. Stir together the sugar, vinegar, and soy sauce until the sugar dissolves. Add the

shallot, chili, and sesame oil, and whisk together with a fork. Transfer to a small serving bowl, cover, and let stand for at least 10 minutes before serving.

5 Remove the pork balls from the steamer, and arrange them on a warmed serving platter. Serve immediately with the sweet chili dipping sauce.

FOOD FACT

These meatballs get their name from the rice coating, which is thought to resemble a lion's mane. Glutinous rice, sometimes labeled "sticky rice," has a high starch content, and the grains stick together when cooked.

HOT-&-SOUR CALAMARI

INGREDIENTS   Serves 4

8 baby squid, cleaned
2 tbsp. dark soy sauce
2 tbsp. hoisin sauce
1 tbsp. lime juice
2 tbsp. dry sherry
1 tbsp. honey
1-in. piece ginger, peeled and
  finely chopped

1 red chili, deseeded and
  finely chopped
1 green chili, deseeded and
  finely chopped
1 tsp. cornstarch
salt and freshly ground black
  pepper
vegetable oil for deep-frying
lime wedges, to garnish

1 Slice open the body of each squid lengthwise, open out, and place on a chopping board with the inside facing up. Using a knife, cut lightly in a crisscross pattern. Cut each one into 4 pieces. Trim the tentacles.

2 Place the soy and hoisin sauces with the lime juice, sherry, honey, ginger, chilies, and cornstarch in a bowl. Season to taste with salt and pepper, and mix together. Add the squid, stir well to coat, then cover and place in the refrigerator to marinate for 1 hour.

3 Tip the squid into a sieve over a small saucepan and strain off the marinade. Scrape any bits of chili or ginger into the saucepan, as they will burn if fried.

4 Fill a deep-fat fryer one -third full with oil, and heat to 350° F. Deep-fry the squid in batches for 2–3 minutes or until golden and crisp. Remove the squid, and drain on paper towels. Keep warm.

5 Bring the marinade to a boil, and let it boil gently for a few seconds. Arrange the squid on a serving dish, and drizzle with the marinade. Garnish with lime wedges and serve immediately.

HELPFUL HINT

It is easy to prepare squid. Rinse well in cold water, then firmly pull apart the head and body; the innards will come away with the head. Remove and discard the transparent beak. Rinse the body pouch thoroughly under cold running water, and peel off the thin layer of dark skin. The tentacles are edible, so cut them away from the head just below the eyes. They can also be deep-fried to be used in this dish, if desired.

AROMATIC QUAIL EGGS

INGREDIENTS

Serves 6

2 tbsp. jasmine tea leaves

24 quail eggs

2 tsp. salt

4 tbsp. dark soy sauce

1 tbsp. dark brown sugar

2 whole star anise

1 cinnamon stick

2 tbsp. sherry vinegar

2 tbsp. Chinese rice wine or dry sherry

2 tbsp. superfine sugar

¼ tsp. Chinese five spice powder

¼ tsp. cornstarch

1 Place the tea leaves in a pitcher and pour in ⅔ cup boiling water. Let stand for 5 minutes, then strain, setting aside the tea and discarding the leaves.

2 Meanwhile, place the eggs in a saucepan with just enough cold water to cover them. Bring to a boil and simmer for 1 minute. Using a slotted spoon, move the eggs, and roll them gently to just crack the shells all over.

3 Add the salt, 2 tablespoons of the soy sauce, the dark brown sugar, star anise, and cinnamon stick to the egg cooking water, and pour in the tea. Bring to a boil, return the eggs to the saucepan, and simmer for 1 minute. Remove from the heat, and leave the eggs for 2 minutes, then remove the eggs and plunge them into cold water. Leave the tea mixture to cool.

4 Return the eggs to the cooled tea mixture, leave for 30 minutes, then drain and remove the shells to reveal the marbling.

5 Pour the remaining soy sauce, the vinegar, and Chinese rice wine or sherry into a small saucepan, and add the superfine sugar and Chinese five spice powder. Blend the cornstarch with 1 tablespoon of cold water, and stir into the soy sauce mixture. Heat until boiling and slightly thickened, stirring continuously. Let cool.

6 Pour the sauce into a small serving dish. Place the eggs in a serving bowl or divide between individual plates and serve with the dipping sauce.

TASTY TIP

This recipe can also be used to marble and flavor ordinary eggs. Allowing nine eggs to serve six people, simmer for 4 minutes in Step 2, and for an additional 4 minutes in Step 3. Leave the eggs to soak, and peel as before, then cut widthwise into quarters when serving.

SPICY SHRIMP IN LETTUCE CUPS

INGREDIENTS   Serves 4

1 lemongrass stalk
1½ cups peeled cooked shrimp
1 tsp. finely grated lime zest
1 red bird's eye chili, deseeded
   and finely chopped
1-in. piece ginger, peeled and
   finely shredded
2 heads romaine lettuce,
   divided into leaves
¼ cup chopped, roasted
   peanuts
2 scallions, trimmed and
   diagonally sliced

sprig of fresh cilantro, to
   garnish

FOR THE COCONUT SAUCE:
2 tbsp. freshly grated coconut
   or unsweetened, shredded
   coconut
1 tbsp. hoisin sauce
1 tbsp. light soy sauce
1 tbsp. Thai fish sauce
1 tbsp. soft golden brown
   sugar

1 Remove 3 or 4 of the tougher outer leaves of the lemongrass, and set aside for another dish. Finely chop the remaining soft center. Place 2 teaspoons of the chopped lemongrass in a bowl with the shrimp, grated lime zest, chili, and ginger. Mix together to coat the shrimp. Cover, and place in the refrigerator to marinate while you make the coconut sauce.

2 For the sauce, place the coconut in a wok and fry for 2–3 minutes or until golden. Remove from the pan and set aside. Add the hoisin, soy, and fish sauces to the pan with the sugar and 4 tablespoons of water. Simmer for 2–3 minutes, then remove from the heat. Let cool.

3 Pour the sauce over the shrimp, add the toasted coconut, and toss to mix together. Divide the shrimp and coconut sauce mixture between the romaine leaves, and arrange on a platter.

4 Sprinkle with the peanuts and scallions, and garnish with a sprig of cilantro. Serve immediately.

HELPFUL HINT

Instead of romaine, use radicchio or endive, available from most supermarkets.

CANTONESE CHICKEN WINGS

INGREDIENTS   Serves 4

3 tbsp. hoisin sauce
2 tbsp. dark soy sauce
1 tbsp. sesame oil
1 garlic clove, peeled and
crushed
1-in. piece ginger, peeled and
finely shredded
1 tbsp. Chinese rice wine or
dry sherry

2 tsp. chili bean sauce
2 tsp. red or white wine
vinegar
2 tbsp. golden brown sugar
2 lbs. large chicken wings
½ cup chopped cashew nuts
2 scallions, trimmed and finely
chopped

1 Preheat the oven to 425° F. Place the hoisin sauce, soy sauce, sesame oil, garlic, ginger, Chinese rice wine or sherry, chili bean sauce, vinegar, and sugar in a small saucepan with 6 tablespoons of water. Bring to a boil, stirring occasionally, then simmer for about 30 seconds. Remove the glaze from the heat.

2 Place the chicken wings in a roasting pan in a single layer. Pour the glaze on top, and stir until the wings are coated thoroughly.

3 Cover the pan loosely with aluminum foil, place in the preheated oven, and roast for 25 minutes. Remove the foil, baste the wings, and cook for an additional 5 minutes.

4 Reduce the oven temperature to 375° F. Turn the wings over, and sprinkle with the chopped cashew nuts and scallions. Return to the oven and cook for 5 minutes or until the nuts are lightly browned, the glaze is sticky, and the wings are tender. Remove from the oven and let stand for 5 minutes before arranging on a warmed platter. Serve immediately with plenty of napkins.

HELPFUL HINT

Chicken wings are regarded as a delicacy in both China and Thailand, and are considered one of the tastiest parts of the bird. If you give your butcher advance notice, he will probably sell them to you very cheaply, as they are often trimmed off and discarded when cutting chickens into portions.

VEGETABLE THAI SPRING ROLLS

INGREDIENTS   Serves 4

2 oz. cellophane vermicelli
4 dried shiitake mushrooms
1 tbsp. peanut oil
2 medium carrots, peeled and
  thinly sliced
⅔ cup snow peas, cut
  lengthwise in fine strips
3 scallions, trimmed and
  chopped
½ cup canned bamboo shoots,
  thinly sliced

½-in. piece ginger, peeled and
  finely shredded
1 tbsp. light soy sauce
1 medium egg, separated
salt and freshly ground black
  pepper
20 spring roll wrappers, each
  about 5 in. square
vegetable oil for deep-frying
scallion tassels, to garnish

1 Place the vermicelli in a bowl and add enough boiling water to cover. Let soak for 5 minutes or until softened, then drain. Cut into 3-in. lengths. Soak the shiitake mushrooms in almost-boiling water for 15 minutes, drain, discard the stalks, and slice thinly.

2 Heat a wok or large skillet, add the peanut oil, and, when hot, add the carrots, and stir-fry for 1 minute. Add the snow peas and scallions, and stir-fry for 2–3 minutes, or until the vegetables are tender. Tip the vegetables into a bowl and leave to cool.

3 Stir the vermicelli and shiitake mushrooms into the cooled vegetables with the bamboo shoots, ginger, soy sauce, and egg yolk. Season to taste with salt and pepper, and mix thoroughly.

4 Brush the edges of a spring roll wrapper with a little beaten egg white. Spoon 2 teaspoons of the vegetable filling onto the wrapper, in a 3-in. log shape, 1 in. from one edge. Fold the wrapper edge over the filling, then fold in the right and left sides. Brush the folded edges with more egg white, and roll up neatly. Place on a greased cookie sheet, seam-side down, and make the rest of the spring rolls.

5 Heat the oil in a heavy-based saucepan or deep-fat fryer to 350° F. Deep-fry the spring rolls, 6 at a time, for 2–3 minutes or until golden brown and crisp. Drain on paper towels and arrange on a warmed platter. Garnish with scallion tassels and serve immediately.

CRISPY SHRIMP WITH CHINESE DIPPING SAUCE

INGREDIENTS   Serves 4

1 lb. medium-size raw shrimp, peeled

¼ tsp. salt

6 tbsp. peanut oil

2 garlic cloves, peeled and finely chopped

1-in. piece fresh ginger, peeled and finely chopped

1 green chili, deseeded and finely chopped

4 stems fresh cilantro, leaves and stems roughly chopped

FOR THE CHINESE DIPPING SAUCE:

3 tbsp. dark soy sauce

3 tbsp. rice wine vinegar

1 tbsp. superfine sugar

2 tbsp. chili oil

2 scallions, finely shredded

1 Using a sharp knife, remove the black veins along the back of the shrimp. Sprinkle the shrimp with the salt, and let stand for 15 minutes. Pat dry on paper towels.

2 Heat a wok or large skillet, add the peanut oil, and, when hot, add the shrimp and stir-fry in 2 batches for about 1 minute or until they turn pink, and are almost cooked. Using a slotted spoon, remove the shrimp, and set aside in a warm oven.

3 Drain the oil from the wok, leaving 1 tablespoon. Add the garlic, ginger, and chili, and cook for about 30 seconds. Add the cilantro, return the shrimp, and stir-fry for 1–2 minutes or until the shrimp are cooked through and the garlic is golden. Turn into a warmed serving dish.

4 For the dipping sauce, beat together the soy sauce, rice vinegar, sugar, and chili oil in a small bowl with a fork. Stir in the scallions. Serve immediately with the hot shrimp.

TASTY TIP

Although you must cook raw shrimp thoroughly, it is equally important not to overcook them, or they will become tough and chewy, and lose their delicate flavor. Stir-fry them until they are pink and opaque, constantly moving them around the pan so that they cook evenly. They will need to be cooked only briefly in Step 3.

POACHED FISH DUMPLINGS WITH CREAMY CHILI SAUCE

INGREDIENTS　　　　　　　　　Serves 4

1 lb. white fish fillet, skinned and boned

1 tsp. dark soy sauce

1 tbsp. cornstarch

1 medium egg yolk

salt and freshly ground black pepper

3 tbsp. freshly chopped cilantro

6½ cups fish stock

FOR THE CREAMY CHILI SAUCE:

2 tsp. peanut oil

2 garlic cloves, peeled and finely chopped

4 scallions, trimmed and finely sliced

2 tbsp. dry sherry

1 tbsp. sweet chili sauce

1 tbsp. light soy sauce

1 tbsp. lemon juice

6 tbsp. crème fraîche or sour cream

TO GARNISH:

sprigs of fresh cilantro

fresh carrot sticks

1 Chop the fish into chunks, and place in a food processor with the soy sauce, cornstarch, and egg yolk. Season to taste with salt and pepper. Blend until fairly smooth. Add the cilantro and process for a few seconds until well mixed. Transfer to a bowl, cover, and chill in the refrigerator for 30 minutes.

2 With damp hands, shape the chilled mixture into walnut-sized balls, and place on a cookie sheet lined with nonstick baking parchment. Chill in the refrigerator for an additional 30 minutes.

3 Pour the stock into a wide saucepan, bring to a boil, then reduce the heat until barely simmering. Add the fish dumplings and poach for 3–4 minutes or until cooked through.

4 Meanwhile, to make the sauce, heat the oil in a small saucepan, add the garlic and scallions, and cook until golden. Stir in the sherry, chili and soy sauces, and lemon juice, then remove immediately from the heat. Stir in the crème fraîche, and season to taste with salt and pepper.

5 Using a slotted spoon, lift the cooked fish dumplings from the stock and place on a warmed serving dish. Drizzle with the sauce, garnish with sprigs of cilantro, and serve immediately.

STEAMED MONKFISH WITH CHILI & GINGER

INGREDIENTS   Serves 4

1½ lbs. skinless monkfish tail
1–2 red chilies
1½-in. piece ginger
1 tsp. sesame oil
4 scallions, trimmed and thinly
  sliced diagonally
2 tbsp. soy sauce

2 tbsp. Chinese rice wine or
  dry sherry
freshly steamed rice, to serve

TO GARNISH:
sprigs of cilantro
lime wedges

1 Place the monkfish on a chopping board. Using a sharp knife, cut down each side of the central bone, and remove. Cut the fish into 1-in. pieces and set aside.

2 Make a slit down the side of each chili, remove and discard the seeds and the membrane, then slice thinly. Peel the ginger, and either chop or shred finely.

3 Brush a large heatproof plate with the sesame oil and arrange the monkfish pieces in one layer on the plate. Sprinkle with the scallions and pour over the soy sauce and Chinese rice wine or sherry.

4 Place a wire rack or inverted ramekin in a large wok. Pour in enough water to come about 1 in. up the side of the wok, and bring to a boil over a high heat.

5 Fold a long piece of aluminum foil lengthwise to about 2–3 in. wide, and lay it over the rack or ramekin. It must extend beyond the plate edge when it is placed in the wok.

6 Place the plate with the monkfish on the rack or ramekin, and cover tightly. Steam over a medium-low heat for 5 minutes or until the fish is tender and opaque. Using the foil as a hammock, lift out the plate. Garnish with sprigs of cilantro and lime wedges, and serve immediately with steamed rice.

FOOD FACT

Chilies transformed Chinese cooking when they were introduced to China about 100 years ago. They are used extensively in Szechuan and Hunan dishes.

RED SHRIMP CURRY WITH JASMINE-SCENTED RICE

INGREDIENTS
Serves 4

½ tbsp. coriander seeds
1 tsp. cumin seeds
1 tsp. black peppercorns
½ tsp. salt
1–2 dried red chilies
2 shallots, peeled and chopped
3–4 garlic cloves
1-in. piece galangal or ginger, peeled and chopped
1 kaffir lime leaf or 1 tsp. kaffir lime zest
½ tsp. red chili powder
½ tbsp. shrimp paste
1–1½ lemongrass stalks, outer leaves removed and thinly sliced
3¼ cups coconut milk

1 red chili, deseeded and thinly sliced
2 tbsp. Thai fish sauce
2 tsp. brown sugar
1 red bell pepper, deseeded and thinly sliced
1¼ lbs. large peeled tiger shrimp
2 fresh lime leaves, shredded (optional)
2 tbsp. fresh mint leaves, shredded
2 tbsp. Thai or Italian basil leaves, shredded
freshly cooked Thai fragrant rice, to serve

1 Using a mortar and pestle or a spice grinder, grind the coriander and cumin seeds, peppercorns, and salt to a fine powder. Add the dried chilies one at a time, and grind to a fine powder.

2 Place the shallots, garlic, galangal or ginger, kaffir lime leaf or zest, chili powder, and shrimp paste in a food processor. Add the ground spices, and process until a thick paste forms. Scrape down the bowl once or twice, adding a few drops of water if the mixture is too thick and not forming a paste. Stir in the lemongrass.

3 Transfer the paste to a large wok, and cook over a medium heat for 2–3 minutes or until fragrant.

4 Stir in the coconut milk, bring to a boil, then lower the heat and simmer for about 10 minutes. Add the chili, fish sauce, sugar, and red bell pepper, and simmer for 15 minutes.

5 Stir in the shrimp and cook for 5 minutes or until the shrimp are pink and tender. Stir in the shredded herbs, heat for an additional minute, and serve immediately with the cooked Thai rice.

THAI SHRIMP & RICE NOODLE SALAD

INGREDIENTS

Serves 4

3 oz. rice vermicelli

1¼ cups snow peas, cut in half crossways

½ cucumber, peeled, deseeded, and diced

2–3 scallions, trimmed and thinly sliced diagonally

16–20 large, cooked tiger shrimp, peeled, with tails left on

2 tbsp. chopped unsalted peanuts or cashews

3 tbsp. Thai fish sauce

1 tbsp. sugar

1-in. piece ginger, peeled and finely chopped

1 red chili, deseeded and thinly sliced

3–4 tbsp. freshly chopped cilantro or mint

TO GARNISH:

lime wedges

sprigs of fresh mint

FOR THE DRESSING:

4 tbsp. freshly squeezed lime juice

1 Place the vermicelli in a bowl, and add enough hot water to cover. Let stand for 5 minutes or until softened. Drain, rinse, then drain again and set aside.

2 Meanwhile, mix all the dressing ingredients in a large bowl until well blended and the sugar has dissolved. Set aside.

3 Bring a medium saucepan of water to a boil. Add the snow peas, return to a boil, and cook for 30–50 seconds. Drain, rinse under cold running water, drain again, and set aside.

4 Stir the cucumber, scallions, and all but 4 of the shrimp into the dressing until coated lightly. Add the snow peas and noodles, and toss until all the ingredients are mixed evenly.

5 Spoon the noodle salad onto warmed individual plates. Sprinkle with peanuts or cashews, and garnish each dish with a shrimp, lime wedge, and sprig of mint.

FOOD FACT

Thai fish sauce, or *nam pla*, adds a richness to many dishes. The fishy flavor virtually disappears when cooked.

THAI CURRIED SEAFOOD

INGREDIENTS
Serves 6-8

2 tbsp. vegetable oil

1 lb. scallops, with coral attached, if desired, halved if large

1 onion, peeled and finely chopped

4 garlic cloves, peeled and finely chopped

2-in. piece ginger, peeled and finely chopped

1–2 red chilies, deseeded and thinly sliced

1–2 tbsp. curry paste (hot or medium, to taste)

1 tsp. ground coriander

1 tsp. ground cumin

1 lemongrass stalk, bruised

8-oz. can chopped tomatoes

½ cup chicken stock or water

2 cups coconut milk

12 live mussels, scrubbed and beards removed

1 lb. peeled cooked shrimp

1 cup frozen or canned crabmeat, drained

2 tbsp. freshly chopped cilantro

freshly shredded coconut, to garnish (optional)

freshly cooked rice or rice noodles, to serve

1 Heat a wok or large skillet, add 1 tablespoon of the oil, and, when hot, add the scallops and stir-fry for 2 minutes or until opaque and firm. Transfer to a plate with any juices.

2 Heat the remaining oil. Add the onion, garlic, ginger, and chilies, and stir-fry for 1 minute or until they begin to soften.

3 Add the curry paste, coriander, cumin, and lemongrass, and stir-fry for 2 minutes. Add the tomatoes and stock, bring to a boil, then simmer for 5 minutes, stirring constantly. Stir in the coconut milk, and simmer for 2 minutes.

4 Stir in the mussels, cover, and simmer for 2 minutes or until they begin to open. Stir in the shrimp, crabmeat, and scallops, with any juices, and cook for 2 minutes or until heated through. Discard the lemongrass and any unopened mussels. Stir in the chopped cilantro. Tip into a large serving dish and garnish with the coconut, if desired. Serve immediately with rice or noodles.

HELPFUL HINT

When preparing live mussels, discard any that do not close when tapped sharply.

FRIED FISH WITH THAI CHILI DIPPING SAUCE

INGREDIENTS   Serves 4

1 large egg white
½ tsp. curry powder or
  turmeric
3–4 tbsp. cornstarch
salt and freshly ground black
  pepper
4 flounder or sole fillets
1¼ cups vegetable oil

FOR THE DIPPING SAUCE:
2 red chilies, deseeded and
  thinly sliced

2 shallots, peeled and finely
  chopped
1 tbsp. freshly squeezed lime
  juice
3 tbsp. Thai fish sauce
1 tbsp. freshly chopped
  cilantro or Thai basil

TO SERVE:
freshly cooked rice
mixed lettuce leaves

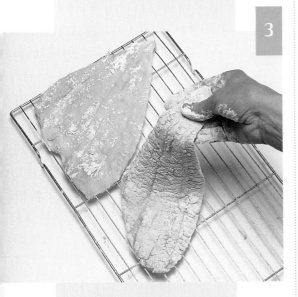

1 To make the dipping sauce, combine all the ingredients in a bowl. Leave for at least 15 minutes.

2 Beat the egg white until frothy, and pour into a shallow dish.

3 Stir the curry powder or turmeric into the cornstarch in a bowl, and season to taste with salt and pepper. Dip each fish fillet in the egg white, dust lightly on both sides with the cornstarch mixture, and place on a wire rack.

4 Heat a wok or large skillet, add the oil, and heat to 350° F. Add 1 or 2 fillets and fry for 5 minutes or until crisp and golden, turning once during cooking.

5 Using a slotted spatula, carefully remove the cooked fish, and drain on paper towels. Keep warm while frying the remaining fillets.

6 Arrange the fillets on warmed individual plates, and serve immediately with the dipping sauce, rice, and salad.

HELPFUL HINT

To prepare fresh chilies, slice them lengthwise with a small, sharp knife, then remove and discard the seeds, unless you want a really fiery dish. Wash your hands thoroughly with soap, as the volatile oils can cause irritation.

Scallops & Shrimp Braised in Lemongrass

INGREDIENTS   Serves 4–6

1 lb. jumbo raw shrimp,
  peeled, with tails left on
¾ lb. scallops, with coral
  attached
2 red chilies, deseeded and
  coarsely chopped
2 garlic cloves, peeled and
  coarsely chopped
4 shallots, peeled
1 tbsp. shrimp paste

2 tbsp. freshly chopped
  cilantro
1¾ cups coconut milk
2–3 lemongrass stalks,
  bruised, outer leaves
  discarded
2 tbsp. Thai fish sauce
1 tbsp. sugar
freshly steamed basmati rice,
  to serve

1 Rinse the shrimp and scallops, and pat dry with paper towels. Using a sharp knife, remove the black veins along the back of the shrimp. Set aside.

2 Place the chilies, garlic, shallots, shrimp paste, and 1 tablespoon of the chopped cilantro in a food processor. Add 1 tablespoon of the coconut milk and 2 tablespoons of water, and blend to form a thick paste. Set aside the chili paste.

3 Pour the remaining coconut milk with 3 tablespoons of water into a large wok or skillet, add the lemongrass, and bring to a boil. Simmer over a medium heat for 10 minutes or until reduced slightly.

4 Stir the chili paste, fish sauce, and sugar into the coconut milk, and continue to simmer for 2 minutes, stirring the mixture occasionally.

5 Add the prepared shrimp and scallops, and simmer gently for 3 minutes, stirring occasionally, or until the shrimp are pink and the scallops are opaque.

6 Remove the lemongrass and stir in the remaining chopped cilantro. Serve immediately, spooned over freshly steamed basmati rice.

FOOD FACT

Shrimp paste is made from fermented, salted shrimp purée that has been dried in the sun. It should be blended with a little water before use. Shrimp sauce, which is not dried, can be substituted.

Fragrant Thai Swordfish with Bell Peppers

INGREDIENTS   Serves 4–6

1¼ lbs. swordfish, cut into 2-in. strips

2 tbsp. vegetable oil

2 lemongrass stalks, peeled, bruised, and cut into 1-in. pieces

1-in. piece ginger, peeled and thinly sliced

4–5 shallots, peeled and thinly sliced

2–3 garlic cloves, peeled and thinly sliced

1 small red bell pepper, deseeded and thinly sliced

1 small yellow bell pepper, deseeded and thinly sliced

2 tbsp. soy sauce

2 tbsp. Chinese rice wine or dry sherry

1–2 tsp. sugar

1 tsp. sesame oil

1 tbsp. Thai or Italian basil, shredded

salt and freshly ground black pepper

1 tbsp. toasted sesame seeds

FOR THE MARINADE:

1 tbsp. soy sauce

1 tbsp. Chinese rice wine or dry sherry

1 tbsp. sesame oil

1 tbsp. cornstarch

1 Blend all the marinade ingredients together in a shallow, nonmetallic baking dish. Add the swordfish, and spoon the marinade over the fish. Cover and leave to marinate in the refrigerator for at least 30 minutes.

2 Using a slotted spatula or spoon, remove the swordfish from the marinade, and drain briefly on paper towels. Heat a wok or large skillet, add the oil, and, when hot, add the swordfish and stir-fry for 2 minutes or until it begins to brown. Remove the swordfish, and drain on paper towels.

3 Add the lemongrass, ginger, shallots, and garlic to the wok, and stir-fry for 30 seconds. Add the bell peppers, soy sauce, Chinese rice wine or sherry, and sugar, and stir-fry for 3–4 minutes.

4 Return the swordfish to the wok, and stir-fry gently for 1–2 minutes or until heated through and coated with the sauce. If necessary, moisten the sauce with a little of the marinade or some water. Stir in the sesame oil and the basil, and season to taste with salt and pepper. Tip into a warmed serving bowl, sprinkle with sesame seeds, and serve immediately.

THAI COCONUT CRAB CURRY

INGREDIENTS

Serves 4–6

1 onion
4 garlic cloves
2-in. piece ginger
2 tbsp. vegetable oil
2–3 tsp. hot curry paste
1¾ cups coconut milk
2 large, dressed crabs, white
and dark meat separated

2 lemongrass stalks, peeled
and bruised
6 scallions, trimmed and
chopped
2 tbsp. freshly shredded Thai
basil or mint, plus extra to
garnish
freshly boiled rice, to serve

1 Peel the onion and chop finely. Peel the garlic, then crush or finely chop. Peel the ginger and either shred or cut into very thin strips. Set aside.

2 Heat a wok or large skillet, add the oil, and when hot, add the onion, garlic, and ginger, and stir-fry for 2 minutes or until the onion is beginning to soften. Stir in the curry paste and stir-fry for 1 minute.

3 Stir the coconut milk into the vegetable mixture with the dark crabmeat. Add the lemongrass, then bring the mixture slowly to a boil, stirring frequently.

4 Add the scallions and simmer gently for 15 minutes or until the sauce has thickened. Remove and discard the lemongrass stalks.

5 Add the white crabmeat and the shredded basil or mint, and stir very gently for 1–2 minutes or until heated through and piping hot. Try to keep the crabmeat from breaking up.

6 Spoon the curry over boiled rice on warmed individual plates, sprinkle with basil or mint leaves, and serve immediately.

FOOD FACT

Lemongrass should be bruised to release its distinctive lemon flavor and scent. This is done by placing it on a chopping board and gently hitting it 2 or 3 times with a rolling pin. For a stronger flavor, the outer leaves can be stripped away and the heart chopped finely. If it is unavailable, a thin strip of lime or lemon zest makes a good alternative.

THAI MARINATED SHRIMP

INGREDIENTS   Serves 4

1½ lbs. jumbo raw shrimp, peeled, with tails left on
2 large eggs
salt
¼ cup cornstarch
vegetable oil for deep-frying
lime wedges, to garnish

FOR THE MARINADE:
2 lemongrass stalks, bruised, outer leaves discarded

2 garlic cloves, peeled and finely chopped
2 shallots, peeled and finely chopped
1 red chili, deseeded and chopped
grated zest and juice of 1 small lime
1¾ cups coconut milk

1 Mix all the marinade ingredients together in a bowl, pressing on the solid ingredients to release their flavors. Season to taste with salt, and set aside.

2 Using a sharp knife, remove the black veins along the back of the shrimp, and pat dry with paper towels. Add the shrimp to the marinade, and stir gently until coated evenly. Leave in the marinade for at least 1 hour, stirring occasionally.

3 Beat the eggs in a deep bowl with a little salt. Place the cornstarch in a shallow bowl. Using a slotted spoon or spatula, transfer the shrimp from the marinade to the cornstarch. Stir gently until the shrimp are coated on all sides, and shake off any excess.

4 Holding each shrimp by its tail, dip it into the beaten egg, then into the cornstarch again, shaking off any excess.

5 Pour enough oil into a large wok to come 2 in. up the sides, and place over a high heat. Working in batches of 5 or 6, deep-fry the shrimp for 2 minutes or until pink and crisp, turning once. Using a slotted spoon, remove and drain on paper towels. Keep warm. Arrange on a warmed serving plate, and garnish with lime wedges. Serve immediately.

TASTY TIP

Use vegetable or peanut oil with a high smoke point. For extra flavor, add 1–2 tablespoons of garlic, chili, or lemon oil. Make sure the oil is hot enough to cook the shrimp quickly, or they will become tough.

WARM LOBSTER SALAD WITH HOT THAI DRESSING

INGREDIENTS

Serves 4

1 orange
¼ cup granulated sugar
2 lettuce hearts, shredded
1 small avocado, peeled and
   thinly sliced
½ cucumber, peeled,
   deseeded, and thinly sliced
1 ripe mango, peeled, pitted,
   and thinly sliced
1 tbsp. butter or vegetable oil
1 large lobster, meat removed
   and cut into bite-size pieces
2 tbsp. Thai basil leaves
4 cooked jumbo shrimp,
   peeled, with tails left on, to
   garnish

FOR THE DRESSING:
1 tbsp. vegetable oil
4–6 scallions, trimmed and
   sliced diagonally into
   2-in. pieces
1-in. piece ginger, peeled and
   finely shredded
1 garlic clove, peeled and
   crushed
grated zest of 1 lime
juice of 2–3 small limes
2 tbsp. Thai fish sauce
1 tbsp. brown sugar
1–2 tsp. sweet chili sauce,
   or to taste
1 tbsp. sesame oil

1 With a sharp knife, julienne the orange rind, then cook in boiling water for 2 minutes.

2 Drain the orange strips, then plunge into cold running water, drain, and return to the saucepan with the sugar and ½ in. of water. Simmer until soft, then add 1 tablespoon of cold water to stop cooking. Remove from the heat and set aside. Arrange the lettuce on four large plates, and arrange the avocado, cucumber, and mango slices over the lettuce.

3 Heat a wok or large skillet, add the butter or oil, and, when hot but not sizzling, add the lobster and stir-fry for 1–2

minutes or until heated through. Remove and drain on paper towels.

4 To make the dressing, heat the vegetable oil in a wok, then add the scallions, ginger, and garlic, and stir-fry for 1 minute. Add the lime zest, lime juice, fish sauce, sugar, and chili sauce. Stir until the sugar dissolves. Remove from the heat, and add the sesame oil with the orange rind and liquid.

5 Arrange the lobster meat over the salad and drizzle with dressing. Sprinkle with basil leaves, garnish with shrimp, and serve immediately.

DEEP-FRIED CRAB WONTONS

INGREDIENTS

Makes 24–30

2 tbsp. sesame oil

6–8 water chestnuts, rinsed, drained and chopped

2 scallions, peeled and finely chopped

½-in. piece ginger, peeled and finely shredded

7-oz. can white crabmeat, drained

¼ cup soy sauce

2 tbsp. rice wine vinegar

½ tsp. dried, crushed chilies

2 tsp. sugar

½ tsp. hot pepper sauce, or to taste

1 tbsp. freshly chopped cilantro or dill

1 large egg yolk

1 packet wonton skins

vegetable oil for deep-frying

lime wedges, to garnish

dipping sauce, to serve (see page 52)

1 Heat a wok or large skillet, add 1 tablespoon of the sesame oil, and, when hot, add the water chestnuts, scallions, and ginger, and stir-fry for 1 minute. Remove from the heat and leave to cool slightly.

2 In a bowl, mix the crabmeat with the soy sauce, rice wine vinegar, crushed chilies, sugar, hot pepper sauce, chopped cilantro or dill, and the egg yolk. Stir in the cooled, stir-fried mixture until well blended.

3 Lay the wonton skins on a work surface and place 1 teaspoonful of the crab mixture on the center of each. Brush the edges of each wonton skin with a little water, and fold up 1 corner to the opposite corner to form a triangle. Press to seal.

4 Bring the 2 corners of the triangle together to meet in the center, brush 1 with a little water, and overlap them, pressing to seal, forming a tortellini shape. Place on a cookie sheet, and continue with the remaining triangles.

5 Pour enough oil into a large wok to come 2 in. up the sides, and place over a high heat. Working in batches of 5 or 6, fry the wontons for 3 minutes or until crisp and golden, turning once or twice.

6 Carefully remove the wontons with a slotted spoon, drain on paper towels, and keep warm. Place on individual warmed serving plates, garnish each dish with a lime wedge, and serve immediately with the dipping sauce.

SZECHUAN CHILI SHRIMP

INGREDIENTS
Serves 4

1 lb. raw jumbo shrimp
2 tbsp. peanut oil
1 onion, peeled and sliced
1 red bell pepper, deseeded
  and cut into strips
1 small red chili, deseeded
  and thinly sliced
2 garlic cloves, peeled and
  finely chopped
2–3 scallions, trimmed and
  diagonally sliced
freshly cooked rice or noodles,
  to serve

sprigs of cilantro or chili
  flowers, to garnish

FOR THE CHILI SAUCE:
1 tbsp. cornstarch
4 tbsp. cold fish stock or water
2 tbsp. soy sauce
2 tbsp. sweet or hot chili
  sauce, or to taste
2 tsp. golden brown sugar

1 Peel the shrimp, leaving the tails attached, if desired. Using a sharp knife, remove the black veins along the back of the shrimp. Rinse and pat dry with paper towels.

2 Heat a wok or large skillet, add the oil, and, when hot, add the onion, bell pepper, and chili, and stir-fry for 4–5 minutes or until the vegetables are tender but retain a bite. Stir in the garlic and cook for 30 seconds. Using a slotted spoon, transfer to a plate and set aside.

3 Add the shrimp to the wok, and stir-fry for 1–2 minutes or until they turn pink and opaque.

4 Blend all the chili sauce ingredients together in a bowl or pitcher, then stir into the

shrimp. Add the vegetables and bring to a boil, stirring constantly. Cook for 1–2 minutes or until the sauce is thickened and the shrimp and vegetables are well coated.

5 Stir in the scallions, tip onto a warmed platter, and garnish with chili flowers or cilantro sprigs. Serve immediately with freshly cooked rice or noodles.

HELPFUL HINT

To make chili flowers, cut off the tips of small chilies and remove the seeds. Snip the chili to make "petals," cutting to within ½ in. of the stalk. Soak them in ice water for about 20 minutes.

STIR-FRIED SALMON WITH PEAS

INGREDIENTS
Serves 4

1 lb. salmon fillet
salt
6 slices bacon
1 tbsp. vegetable oil
¼ cup chicken or fish stock
2 tbsp. dark soy sauce
2 tbsp. Chinese rice wine or
dry sherry
1 tsp. sugar

heaping ½ cup frozen peas,
thawed
1–2 tbsp. freshly shredded
mint
1 tsp. cornstarch
sprigs of fresh mint, to garnish
freshly cooked noodles, to
serve

1 Wipe and skin the salmon fillet, and remove any pin bones. Slice into 1-in. strips, place on a plate, and sprinkle with salt. Leave for 20 minutes, then pat dry with paper towels and set aside.

2 Remove any cartilage from the bacon, dice, and set aside.

3 Heat a wok or large skillet over a high heat, then add the oil, and, when hot, add the bacon and stir-fry for 3 minutes or until crisp and golden. Push to one side and add the strips of salmon. Stir-fry gently for 2 minutes or until the flesh is opaque.

4 Pour the chicken or fish stock, soy sauce, and Chinese rice wine or sherry into the wok, then stir in the sugar, peas, and freshly shredded mint.

5 Blend the cornstarch with 1 tablespoon of water to form a smooth paste, and stir into the sauce. Bring to a boil, reduce the heat, and simmer for 1 minute or until slightly thickened and smooth. Garnish and serve immediately with noodles.

HELPFUL HINT

Sprinkling salmon with salt draws out some of the juices and makes the flesh firmer, so that it remains whole when cooked. Prior to cooking, pat the strips with paper towels to remove as much of the salty liquid as possible. Dark soy sauce is used in this recipe, as it is slightly less salty than the light version. To reduce the salt content further, cook the noodles in plain boiling water without added salt.

CHINESE STEAMED FISH WITH BLACK BEANS

INGREDIENTS

Serves 4

2½ lbs. sea bass, grouper, or flounder, cleaned, with heads and tails left on

1–2 tbsp. rice wine or dry sherry

1½ tbsp. peanut oil

2–3 tbsp. fermented black beans, rinsed and drained

1 garlic clove, peeled and finely chopped

½-in. piece ginger, peeled and finely chopped

4 scallions, trimmed and thinly sliced diagonally

2–3 tbsp. soy sauce

½ cup fish or chicken stock

1–2 tbsp. sweet Chinese chili sauce, or to taste

2 tsp. sesame oil

sprigs of cilantro, to garnish

1 Using a sharp knife, cut 3–4 deep diagonal slashes along both sides of the fish. Sprinkle the Chinese rice wine or sherry inside and over the fish, and gently rub into the skin on both sides.

2 Lightly brush a heatproof plate, large enough to fit into a large wok or skillet, with a little of the peanut oil. Place the fish on the plate, curving the fish as necessary, then leave for 20 minutes.

3 Place a wire rack or inverted ramekin in the wok and pour in enough water to come about 1 in. up the side. Bring to a boil over a high heat.

4 Carefully place the plate with the fish on the rack or ramekin, cover, and steam for 12–15 minutes or until the fish is tender, and the flesh is opaque when pierced near the bone with a knife.

5 Remove the plate with the fish from the wok, and keep warm. Remove the rack or ramekin from the wok, and pour off the water. Return the wok to the heat, add the remaining peanut oil, and swirl to coat the bottom and side. Add the black beans, garlic, and ginger, and stir-fry for 1 minute.

6 Add the scallions, soy sauce, fish or chicken stock, and boil for 1 minute. Stir in the chili sauce and sesame oil, then pour the sauce over the cooked fish. Garnish with sprigs of cilantro and serve immediately.

SWEET-&-SOUR FISH

INGREDIENTS   Serves 4

1 small carrot, thinly sliced
1 small red or green bell
  pepper
¾ cup snow peas, cut in half
  diagonally
⅔ cup frozen peas, thawed
2–3 scallions, trimmed and
  sliced diagonally into
  2-in. pieces
1 lb. small, thin, skinless
  flounder fillets
1½–2 tbsp. cornstarch
vegetable oil for frying
sprigs of fresh cilantro,
  to garnish

**FOR THE SWEET-&-SOUR
SAUCE:**
2 tsp. cornstarch
1¼ cups fish or chicken stock
1½-in. piece ginger, peeled and
  finely sliced
2 tbsp. soy sauce
2 tbsp. rice wine vinegar or
  dry sherry
2 tbsp. ketchup or tomato
  paste
2 tbsp. Chinese rice vinegar or
  cider vinegar
1½ tbsp. golden brown sugar

1 Make the sauce. Place the cornstarch in a saucepan, and gradually whisk in the stock. Stir in the remaining sauce ingredients and bring to a boil, stirring, until the sauce thickens. Simmer for 2 minutes, then remove from the heat and set aside.

2 Bring a saucepan of water to a boil. Add the carrot, return to a boil, and cook for 3 minutes. Add the bell pepper and cook for 1 minute. Add the snow peas and peas, and cook for 30 seconds. Drain, rinse under cold running water, and drain again, then add to the sweet-&-sour sauce with the scallions.

3 Using a sharp knife, make crisscross slashes across the top of each fish fillet, then lightly coat on both sides with the cornstarch.

4 Pour enough oil into a large wok to come 2 in. up the side. Heat to 375° F or until a cube of bread browns in 30 seconds. Fry the fish fillets, 2 at a time, for 3–5 minutes or until crisp and golden, turning once. Using a fish slice, remove and drain on paper towels. Keep warm.

5 Bring the sweet-&-sour sauce to a boil, stirring constantly. Arrange the fish fillets on a warmed platter, and pour over the hot sauce. Garnish with sprigs of cilantro, and serve immediately.

FISH BALLS IN HOT YELLOW BEAN SAUCE

INGREDIENTS　　　　　　　　　　Serves 4

1 lb. skinless white fish fillets, cut into pieces
½ tsp. salt
1 tbsp. cornstarch
2 scallions, trimmed and chopped
1 tbsp. freshly chopped cilantro
1 tsp. soy sauce
1 medium egg white
freshly ground black pepper
sprig of tarragon, to garnish
freshly cooked rice, to serve

FOR THE YELLOW BEAN SAUCE:
5 tbsp. fish or chicken stock
1–2 tsp. yellow bean sauce
2 tbsp. soy sauce
1–2 tbsp. Chinese rice wine or dry sherry
1 tsp. chili bean sauce, or to taste
1 tsp. sesame oil
1 tsp. sugar (optional)

1 Put the fish pieces, salt, cornstarch, scallions, cilantro, soy sauce, and egg white into a food processor. Season to taste with pepper, then blend until a smooth paste forms, scraping down the sides of the bowl occasionally.

2 With dampened hands, shape the mixture into 1-in. balls. Transfer to a baking sheet, and chill in the refrigerator for at least 30 minutes.

3 Bring a large saucepan of water to simmering point. Working in 2 or 3 batches, drop in the fish balls, and poach gently for 3–4 minutes or until they float to the top. Transfer to paper towels to drain.

4 Put all the sauce ingredients in a wok or large skillet, and bring to a boil. Add the fish balls to the sauce, and stir gently for 2–3 minutes until piping hot. Transfer to a warmed serving dish, garnish with sprigs of tarragon, and serve immediately with freshly cooked rice.

FOOD FACT

Yellow bean and brown bean sauces, made from fermented soybeans, have a strong salty taste. If you buy yellow bean sauce in a can, transfer it to a glass container and store in the refrigerator; it will keep for up to a year.

STEAMED WHOLE TROUT WITH GINGER & SCALLION

INGREDIENTS
Serves 4

2 1-lb. whole trout, gutted, with heads removed
coarse sea salt
2 tbsp. peanut oil
½ tbsp. soy sauce
1 tbsp. sesame oil
2 garlic cloves, peeled and thinly sliced
1-in. piece ginger, peeled and thinly slivered
2 scallions, trimmed and thinly sliced diagonally

TO GARNISH:
chive leaves
lemon slices

TO SERVE:
freshly cooked rice
Asian salad, to serve

1 Wipe the fish inside and out with paper towels, then rub with salt inside and out, and leave for about 20 minutes. Pat dry with paper towels.

2 Set a steamer rack or inverted ramekin in a large wok, and pour in enough water to come about 2 in. up the side of the wok. Bring to a boil.

3 Brush a heatproof dinner plate with a little of the peanut oil, and place the fish on the plate with the tails pointing in opposite directions. Place the plate on the rack, cover tightly, and simmer over a medium heat for 10–12 minutes or until tender, and the flesh is opaque near the bone.

4 Carefully transfer the plate to a heatproof surface. Sprinkle with the soy sauce, and keep warm.

5 Pour the water out of the wok and return to the heat. Add the remaining peanut and sesame oils, and, when hot, add the garlic, ginger, and scallions, and stir-fry for 2 minutes or until golden. Pour over the fish, garnish with chive leaves and lemon slices, and serve immediately with rice and an Asian salad.

FOOD FACT

There are 3 types of trout: rainbow trout, golden trout, and brown trout.

STIR-FRIED CALAMARI WITH ASPARAGUS

INGREDIENTS   Serves 4

1 lb. squid, cleaned and cut into ½-in. rings

½ lb. fresh asparagus, sliced diagonally into 2½-in. pieces

2 tbsp. peanut oil

2 garlic cloves, peeled and thinly sliced

1-in. piece ginger, peeled and thinly sliced

½ lb. bok choy, trimmed

5 tbsp. chicken stock

2 tbsp. soy sauce

2 tbsp. oyster sauce

1 tbsp. Chinese rice wine or dry sherry

2 tsp cornstarch, blended with 1 tbsp. water

1 tbsp. sesame oil

1 tbsp. toasted sesame seeds

freshly cooked rice, to serve

1 Bring a medium saucepan of water to a boil over a high heat. Add the squid, return to a boil, and cook for 30 seconds. Using a wide wok strainer or slotted spoon, transfer to a colander, drain, and set aside.

2 Add the asparagus to the boiling water, and blanch for 2 minutes. Drain and set aside.

3 Heat a wok or large skillet, add the peanut oil, and, when hot, add the garlic and ginger, and stir-fry for 30 seconds. Add the bok choy, stir-fry for 1–2 minutes, then pour in the stock and cook for 1 minute.

4 Blend the soy sauce, oyster sauce, and Chinese rice wine or sherry in a bowl or pitcher, then pour into the wok.

5 Add the squid and asparagus to the wok, and stir-fry for 1 minute. Stir the blended cornstarch into the wok. Cook, stirring, for 1 minute or until the sauce thickens and all the ingredients are well coated.

6 Stir in the sesame oil, give a final stir, and turn into a warmed serving dish. Sprinkle with the toasted sesame seeds, and serve immediately with freshly cooked rice.

TASTY TIP

Bok choy is a member of the cabbage family. If available, use baby bok choy or Shanghai bok choy, which is slightly smaller and more delicately flavored.

CHINESE FIVE SPICE MARINATED SALMON

INGREDIENTS — Serves 4

1½ lbs. skinless salmon fillet, cut into 1-in. strips
2 medium egg whites
1 tbsp. cornstarch
vegetable oil for frying
4 scallions, cut diagonally into 2-in. pieces
½ cup fish stock
lime or lemon wedges, to garnish

FOR THE MARINADE:
3 tbsp. soy sauce
3 tbsp. Chinese rice wine or dry sherry
2 tsp. sesame oil
1 tbsp. brown sugar
1 tbsp. lime or lemon juice
1 tsp. Chinese five spice powder
2–3 dashes hot pepper sauce

1 Combine the marinade ingredients in a shallow nonmetallic baking dish until well blended. Add the salmon strips, and stir gently to coat. Leave to marinate in the refrigerator for 20–30 minutes.

2 Using a slotted spoon or fish slice, remove the salmon pieces, drain on paper towels, and pat dry. Set aside the marinade.

3 Beat the egg whites with the cornstarch to make a batter. Add the salmon strips, and stir into the batter until coated completely.

4 Pour enough oil into a large wok to come 2 in. up the side, and place over a high heat. Working in 2 or 3 batches, add the salmon strips, and cook for 1–2 minutes or until golden.

Remove from the wok with a slotted spoon, and drain on paper towels. Set aside.

5 Discard the hot oil and wipe the wok clean. Add the marinade, scallions, and stock to the wok. Bring to a boil, and simmer for 1 minute. Add the salmon strips, and stir gently until coated in the sauce. Spoon into a warmed, shallow serving dish, garnish with the lime or lemon wedges, and serve immediately.

HELPFUL HINT

If desired, marinate the salmon for 4–6 hours for a stronger, more intense flavor.

SCALLOPS WITH BLACK BEAN SAUCE

INGREDIENTS
Serves 4

1½ lbs. scallops, with their coral

2 tbsp. vegetable oil

2–3 tbsp. Chinese fermented black beans, rinsed, drained, and coarsely chopped

2 garlic cloves, peeled and finely chopped

1½-in. piece ginger, peeled and finely chopped

4–5 scallions, thinly sliced diagonally

2–3 tbsp. soy sauce

1½ tbsp. Chinese rice wine or dry sherry

1–2 tsp. sugar

1 tbsp. fish stock or water

2–3 dashes hot pepper sauce

1 tbsp. sesame oil

freshly cooked noodles, to serve

1 Pat the scallops dry with paper towels. Carefully separate the orange coral from the scallop. Peel off and discard the membrane and thick, opaque muscle that attaches the coral to the scallop. Cut any large scallops crosswise in half, leaving the corals whole.

2 Heat a wok or large skillet, add the oil, and, when hot, add the white scallop meat and stir-fry for 2 minutes or until just beginning to brown on the edges. Using a slotted spoon or spatula, transfer to a plate. Set aside.

3 Add the black beans, garlic, and ginger, and stir-fry for 1 minute. Add the scallions, soy sauce, Chinese rice wine or sherry, sugar, fish stock or water, hot pepper sauce, and the corals, and stir until mixed.

4 Return the scallops and juices to the wok, and stir gently for 3 minutes or until the scallops and corals are cooked through. Add a little more stock or water if necessary. Stir in the sesame oil, and turn into a heated serving dish. Serve immediately with noodles.

FOOD FACT

Fermented black beans are also known as "salted black beans" or, simply, "black beans." These small black soybeans need rinsing briefly, then should be crushed or coarsely chopped to release their tangy flavor.

PORK FRIED NOODLES

INGREDIENTS   Serves 4

¼ lb. dried, thread egg noodles
1 cup broccoli florets
4 tbsp. peanut oil
¾ lb. pork tenderloin, cut into slices
3 tbsp. soy sauce
1 tbsp. lemon juice
pinch of sugar
1 tsp. chili sauce
1 tbsp. sesame oil
1-in. piece ginger, peeled and sliced
1 garlic clove, peeled and chopped

1 green chili, deseeded and sliced
¾ cup snow peas, halved
2 medium eggs, lightly beaten
8-oz. can water chestnuts, drained and sliced

TO GARNISH:
radish rose
scallion tassels

1 Place the noodles in a bowl and cover with boiling water. Let stand for 20 minutes, stirring occasionally, or until tender. Drain and set aside. Meanwhile, blanch the broccoli in a saucepan of lightly salted, boiling water for 2 minutes. Drain under cold running water, and set aside.

2 Heat a large wok or skillet, add the peanut oil, and heat until just smoking. Add the pork and stir-fry for 5 minutes or until browned. Using a slotted spoon, remove the pork slices, and set aside.

3 Mix together the soy sauce, lemon juice, sugar, chili sauce, and sesame oil, and set aside.

4 Add the ginger to the wok and stir-fry for 30 seconds. Add the garlic and chili, and stir-fry for 30 seconds. Add the broccoli, and stir-fry for 3 minutes. Stir in the snow peas, pork, and noodles with the beaten eggs and water chestnuts, and stir-fry for 5 minutes or until heated through. Pour over the chili sauce, toss well, and turn into a warmed serving dish. Garnish and serve immediately.

FOOD FACT

Make radish roses by cutting the tops and bottoms off the radishes. Make small slits from the top to the base, then plunge the radishes into ice water for 30 minutes.

HOISIN PORK

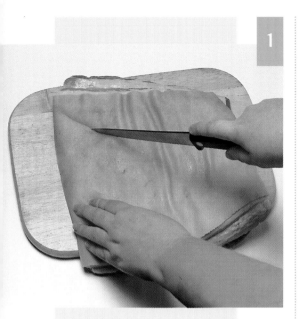

INGREDIENTS   Serves 4

3 lb. piece lean pork sparerib,
  boned
sea salt
2 tsp. Chinese five spice
  powder
2 garlic cloves, peeled and
  chopped

1 tsp. sesame oil
4 tbsp. hoisin sauce
1 tbsp. honey
assorted lettuce leaves, to
  garnish

1 Preheat the oven to 400° F. Using a sharp knife, cut the pork skin in a crisscross pattern, making sure not to cut all the way through into the flesh. Rub the salt evenly over the skin, and let stand for 30 minutes.

2 Meanwhile, mix together the five spice powder, garlic, sesame oil, hoisin sauce, and honey until smooth. Rub the mixture evenly over the pork skin. Place the pork on a plate and chill in the refrigerator to marinate for up to 6 hours.

3 Place the pork on a wire rack set inside a roasting pan and roast the pork in the preheated oven for 1–1¼ hours or until the pork is very crisp, and the juices run clear when the meat is pierced with a skewer.

4 Remove the pork from the oven, leave to rest for 15 minutes, then cut into strips. Arrange on a warmed serving platter. Garnish with lettuce leaves and serve immediately.

FOOD FACT

Sparerib is a cut of pork belly, including the lower part of the ribs, and the thin belly. It has roughly the same proportion of fat to lean meat in thin, alternate layers. Here, it is well cooked so that the meat is tender, and the fat golden brown and crispy. Pork is the most popular meat in China, and in rural parts nearly every family will keep a pig.

COCONUT BEEF

INGREDIENTS   Serves 4

1 lb. sirloin steak
4 tbsp. peanut oil
2 bunches scallions, trimmed
  and thickly sliced
1 red chili, deseeded and
  chopped
1 garlic clove, peeled and
  chopped
1-in. piece ginger, peeled and
  sliced
¼ lb. shiitake mushrooms

¾ cup coconut cream
⅔ cup chicken stock
4 tbsp. freshly chopped
  cilantro
salt and freshly ground black
  pepper
freshly cooked rice, to serve

1 Trim off any fat or gristle from the steak, and cut into thin strips. Heat a wok or large skillet, add 2 tablespoons of the oil, and heat until just smoking. Add the beef and cook for 5–8 minutes, turning occasionally, until browned on all sides. Using a slotted spoon, transfer the beef to a plate, and keep warm.

2 Add the remaining oil to the wok and heat until almost smoking. Add the scallions, chili, garlic, and ginger, and cook for 1 minute, stirring occasionally. Add the mushrooms and stir-fry for 3 minutes. Using a slotted spoon, transfer the mushroom mixture to a plate, and keep warm.

3 Return the beef to the wok, and pour in the coconut cream and stock. Bring to a boil, and simmer for 3–4 minutes or until the juices are slightly reduced and the beef is tender.

4 Return the mushroom mixture to the wok, and heat through. Stir in the chopped cilantro, and season to taste with salt and pepper. Serve immediately with freshly cooked rice.

FOOD FACT

Shiitake mushrooms, which grow naturally on decaying trees, are now cultivated on the *shii* tree, hence their name. Here they are used fresh, but are often used dried. To prepare fresh mushrooms, wipe with damp paper towels to remove any dirt, remove and discard the tough stalks, and slice the caps, if large.

PORK MEATBALLS WITH VEGETABLES

INGREDIENTS Serves 4

1 lb. ground pork
2 tbsp. freshly chopped
  cilantro
2 garlic cloves, peeled and
  chopped
1 tbsp. light soy sauce
salt and freshly ground black
  pepper
2 tbsp. peanut oil
1-in. piece ginger, peeled and
  thinly sliced
1 red bell pepper, deseeded
  and cut into chunks

1 green bell pepper, deseeded
  and cut into chunks
2 zucchini, trimmed and cut
  into sticks
¼ lb. baby corn, halved
  lengthwise
3 tbsp. light soy sauce
1 tsp. sesame oil
cilantro, to garnish
freshly cooked noodles, to
  serve

1 Mix together the ground pork, the chopped cilantro, half the garlic, and the soy sauce, then season to taste with salt and pepper. Divide into 20 portions and roll into balls. Place on a baking sheet, cover with plastic wrap, and chill in the refrigerator for at least 30 minutes.

2 Heat a wok or large skillet, add the peanut oil, and, when hot, add the meatballs and cook for 8–10 minutes or until the pork balls are browned all over, turning occasionally. Using a slotted spoon, transfer the balls to a plate, and keep warm.

3 Add the ginger and remaining garlic to the wok, and stir-fry for 30 seconds. Add the red and bell green peppers, and stir-fry for 5 minutes. Add the zucchini and baby corn, and stir-fry for 3 minutes.

4 Return the meatballs to the wok, add the soy sauce and sesame oil, and stir-fry for 1 minute or until heated through. Garnish with cilantro and serve immediately on a bed of noodles.

HELPFUL HINT

Chilling firms the meatballs and helps to keep them from breaking up during cooking. If you find it easier, cook the meatballs in 2 batches.

SPICY PORK

INGREDIENTS   Serves 4

4 tbsp. peanut oil

1-in. piece ginger, peeled and thinly sliced

1 garlic clove, peeled and chopped

2 medium carrots, peeled and thinly sliced

1 medium eggplant, trimmed and cubed

1½ lbs. pork fillet, thickly sliced

1¾ cups coconut milk

2 tbsp. Thai red curry paste

4 tbsp. Thai fish sauce

2 tsp. superfine sugar

8-oz. can bamboo shoots in brine, drained and sliced

salt, to taste

lime zest, to garnish

freshly cooked rice, to serve

1 Heat a wok or large skillet, add 2 tablespoons of the oil, and, when hot, add the ginger, garlic, carrots, and eggplant, and stir-fry for 3 minutes. Using a slotted spoon, transfer to a plate, and keep warm.

2 Add the remaining oil to the wok, heat until smoking, then add the pork, and stir-fry for 5–8 minutes or until browned all over. Transfer to a plate and keep warm. Wipe the wok clean.

3 Pour half the coconut milk into the wok, stir in the red curry paste, and bring to a boil. Boil rapidly for 4 minutes, stirring occasionally, or until the sauce is reduced by half.

4 Add the fish sauce and sugar to the wok, and bring back to a boil. Return the pork and vegetables to the wok, along with the bamboo shoots. Return to a boil, then simmer for 4 minutes.

5 Stir in the remaining coconut milk, and season to taste with salt. Simmer for 2 minutes or until heated through. Garnish with lime zest, and serve immediately with rice.

FOOD FACT

Coconut milk is the thick, sweet liquid produced by pouring boiling water over grated coconut, then squeezing it out. Using twice as much water by volume as grated coconut produces "milk" of normal thickness. Using equal quantities produces "cream," but this is not the same as store-bought coconut cream.

PORK WITH TOFU & COCONUT

INGREDIENTS   Serves 4

1⅓ cups unsalted cashews
1 tbsp. ground coriander
1 tbsp. ground cumin
2 tsp. hot chili powder
1-in. piece ginger, peeled and chopped
1 tbsp. oyster sauce
4 tbsp. peanut oil
1¾ cups coconut milk
6 oz. rice noodles
1 lb. pork tenderloin, thickly sliced

1 red chili, deseeded and sliced
1 green chili, deseeded and sliced
1 bunch scallions, trimmed and thickly sliced
3 tomatoes, roughly chopped
3 oz. tofu, drained
2 tbsp. freshly chopped cilantro
2 tbsp. freshly chopped mint
salt and freshly ground black pepper

1 Place the cashews, coriander, cumin, chili powder, ginger, and oyster sauce in a food processor, and blend until well ground. Heat a wok or large skillet, add 2 tablespoons of the oil, and, when hot, add the cashew mixture and stir-fry for 1 minute. Stir in the coconut milk, bring to a boil, then simmer for 1 minute. Pour into a small pitcher and set aside. Wipe the wok clean.

2 Meanwhile, place the rice noodles in a bowl, cover with boiling water, let stand for 5 minutes, then drain thoroughly.

3 Reheat the wok, add the remaining oil, and, when hot, add the pork and stir-fry for 5 minutes or until browned all over. Add the chilies and scallions, and stir-fry for 2 minutes.

4 Add the tomatoes and tofu to the wok with the noodles and coconut mixture, and stir-fry for an additional 2 minutes or until heated through, being careful not to break up the tofu. Sprinkle with the chopped cilantro and mint, season to taste with salt and pepper, and stir. Tip into a warmed serving dish, and serve immediately.

HELPFUL HINT

Dried rice noodles are white and opaque, and come in a variety of shapes. Most types need to be soaked briefly in boiling water before use, but always check the package instructions, as soaking times may vary.

CHILI BEEF

INGREDIENTS

Serves 4

1¼ lbs. steak
2 tbsp. peanut oil
2 carrots, peeled and thinly
  sliced
¾ cup shredded snow peas
2 cups bean sprouts
1 green chili, deseeded and
  chopped

2 tbsp. sesame seeds
freshly cooked rice, to serve

FOR THE MARINADE:
1 garlic clove, peeled and
  chopped
3 tbsp. soy sauce
1 tbsp. sweet chili sauce
4 tbsp. peanut oil

1 Using a sharp knife, trim the steak, discarding any fat or gristle, then cut into thin strips, and place in a shallow dish. Combine all the marinade ingredients in a bowl, and pour over the steak. Turn the beef in the marinade until coated evenly, cover with plastic wrap, and leave to marinate in the refrigerator for at least 30 minutes.

2 Heat a wok or large skillet, add the peanut oil, and heat until almost smoking, then add the carrots and stir-fry for 3–4 minutes or until softened. Add the snow peas and stir-fry for an additional 1 minute. Using a slotted spoon, transfer the vegetables to a plate, and keep warm.

3 Lift the steak strips from the marinade, shaking to remove any excess. Set aside the marinade. Add the steak to the wok and stir-fry for 3 minutes or until browned all over.

4 Return the stir-fried vegetables to the wok, along with the bean sprouts, chili, and sesame seeds, and cook for 1 minute. Stir in the marinade, and stir-fry for 1–2 minutes or until heated through. Tip into a warmed serving dish, or spoon onto individual plates, and serve immediately with freshly cooked rice.

FOOD FACT

Chilies have become a popular Chinese ingredient, especially in Szechuan cuisine. Chili sauce is a mixture of crushed chilies, plums, vinegar, and salt. It is available in several strengths: extra hot, hot, or sweet, which is the mildest version. Chili sauce may be used as a marinade or as a dip.

PORK WITH BLACK BEAN SAUCE

INGREDIENTS

Serves 4

1½ lbs. pork tenderloin
4 tbsp. light soy sauce
2 tbsp. peanut oil
1 garlic clove, peeled and
    chopped
1-in. piece ginger, peeled and
    thinly sliced
1 large carrot, peeled and
    sliced

1 red bell pepper, deseeded
    and sliced
1 green bell pepper, deseeded
    and sliced
6 oz. jar black bean sauce
salt
fresh chives, to garnish
freshly steamed rice, to serve

1 Using a sharp knife, trim the pork, discarding any fat or sinew, and cut into bite-size chunks. Place in a large, shallow dish and add the soy sauce. Turn to coat evenly, cover with plastic wrap, and leave to marinate for at least 30 minutes in the refrigerator. When ready to use, lift the pork from the marinade, shaking off as much marinade as possible, and pat dry with paper towels. Set aside the marinade.

2 Heat a wok, add the peanut oil, and, when hot, add the chopped garlic and ginger, and stir-fry for 30 seconds. Add the carrot and the bell peppers, and stir-fry for 3–4 minutes or until just softened.

3 Add the pork to the wok, and stir-fry for 5–7 minutes or until browned all over and tender. Pour in the marinade and black bean sauce. Bring to a boil, stirring constantly until well blended, then simmer for 1 minute, until heated through. Tip into a warmed serving dish, or spoon on to individual plates. Garnish with chives, and serve immediately with steamed rice.

TASTY TIP

Before cooking the pork, shake off as much marinade as possible, then pat the meat dry with paper towels to absorb any moisture. This will ensure that the meat is fried in the hot oil and browns properly. If too much liquid is added with the meat, it tends to stew in the juices.

PORK SPRING ROLLS

INGREDIENTS   Serves 4

¼ lb. pork tenderloin
2 tbsp. light soy sauce
1 cup peanut oil
1 medium carrot, peeled and
  thinly sliced
1 cup wiped and sliced button
  mushrooms
4 scallions, trimmed and thinly
  sliced

1½ cups bean sprouts
1 garlic clove, peeled and
  chopped
1 tbsp. dark soy sauce
12 large sheets phyllo pastry,
  folded in half
scallion curls, to garnish
Chinese-style dipping sauce,
  to serve

1 Trim the pork, discarding any sinew or fat, and cut into very fine strips. Place in a small bowl, pour over the light soy sauce, and stir until well coated. Cover with plastic wrap, and leave to marinate in the refrigerator for at least 30 minutes.

2 Heat a wok or large skillet, add 1 tablespoon of the oil, and, when hot, add the carrot and mushrooms, and stir-fry for 3 minutes or until softened. Add the scallions, bean sprouts, and garlic, stir-fry for 2 minutes, then transfer the vegetables to a bowl and set aside.

3 Drain the pork well, add to the wok, and stir-fry for 2–4 minutes or until browned. Add the pork to the vegetables, and leave to cool. Stir in the dark soy sauce, and mix the filling well.

4 Lay the folded phyllo pastry sheets on a work surface. Divide the filling between the sheets, placing it at one end. Brush the phyllo edges with water, then fold the sides over, and roll up.

5 Heat the remaining oil in a large wok to 350° F, and cook the spring rolls in batches for 2–3 minutes or until golden, turning occasionally during cooking. Using a slotted spoon, remove and drain on paper towels. Garnish with scallion curls, and serve immediately with a Chinese-style dipping sauce.

TASTY TIP

To make a dipping sauce, blend together 2 tablespoons dark soy sauce, 1 tablespoon Chinese rice wine or dry sherry, 2 teaspoons chili bean sauce, 2 teaspoons toasted sesame seed oil, and 1 teaspoon superfine sugar. Stir in 1 very finely chopped scallion.

SPECIAL FRIED RICE

INGREDIENTS   Serves 4

2 tbsp. butter

4 medium eggs, beaten

4 tbsp. vegetable oil

1 bunch scallions, trimmed
and shredded

2½ cups diced, cooked ham

1½ cups large cooked shrimp,
with tails left on

½ cup peas, thawed if frozen

7-oz. can water chestnuts,
drained and roughly
chopped

3 cups cooked long-grain rice

3 tbsp. dark soy sauce

1 tbsp. dry sherry

2 tbsp. freshly chopped
cilantro

salt and freshly ground black
pepper

1 Melt the butter in a wok or large skillet, and pour in half the beaten egg. Cook for 4 minutes, drawing the edges of the omelette in to allow the uncooked egg to set into a round shape. Using a fish slice, lift the omelette from the wok, and roll into a sausage shape. Leave to cool completely, then, using a sharp knife, slice the omelette into rings.

2 Wipe the wok with paper towels, and return to the heat. Add the oil, and, when hot, add the scallions, ham, shrimp, peas, and chopped water chestnuts, and stir-fry for 2 minutes. Add the rice and stir-fry for an additional 3 minutes.

3 Add the remaining beaten eggs and stir-fry for 3 minutes or until the egg has scrambled and set. Stir in the soy sauce, sherry, and chopped cilantro. Season to taste with salt and pepper, and heat through. Add the omelette rings, and gently stir without breaking up the egg too much. Serve immediately.

HELPFUL HINT

In Chinese cuisine, rice is always cooked by the absorption method, rather than in large quantities of boiling water, so that all the flavor and nutrients are retained. Long-grain rice is popular, but Thai fragrant rice is served on special occasions. Medium and short-grain rices are also used in savory dishes. Long-grain rice absorbs 1½ to 3 times its volume in water, so you will need to start with about 1 cup uncooked rice for this dish.

BEEF & BABY CORN STIR-FRY

INGREDIENTS   Serves 4

3 tbsp. light soy sauce
1 tbsp. honey, warmed
1 lb. beef steak, trimmed and
  thinly sliced
6 tbsp. peanut oil
¼ lb. shiitake mushrooms,
  wiped and halved
2 cups bean sprouts, rinsed
1-in. piece ginger, peeled and
  thinly sliced
¾ cup snow peas, halved
  lengthwise
1 cup broccoli, trimmed and
  cut into florets

1 medium carrot, peeled and
  thinly sliced
¼ lb. baby corn, halved
  lengthwise
¼ head Chinese cabbage,
  shredded
1 tbsp. chili sauce
3 tbsp. black bean sauce
1 tbsp. dry sherry
freshly cooked noodles, to
  serve

1 Mix together the soy sauce and honey in a shallow dish. Add the sliced steak, and turn to coat evenly. Cover with plastic wrap, and leave to marinate for at least 30 minutes, turning occasionally.

2 Heat a wok or large skillet, add 2 tablespoons of the oil, and heat until just smoking. Add the mushrooms and stir-fry for 1 minute. Add the bean sprouts and stir-fry for 1 minute. Using a slotted spoon, transfer the mushroom mixture to a plate, and keep warm.

3 Drain the steak, setting aside the marinade. Reheat the wok, pour in 2 tablespoons of the oil, and heat until smoking. Add the steak and stir-fry for 4 minutes or until browned. Move to a plate, and keep warm.

4 Add the remaining oil to the wok, and heat until just smoking. Add the ginger, snow peas, broccoli, carrots, the baby corn, and the shredded Chinese cabbage, and stir-fry for 3 minutes. Stir in the chili and black bean sauces, the sherry, marinade, and steak and mushroom mixture. Stir-fry for 2 minutes, then serve immediately with freshly cooked noodles.

TASTY TIP

You could use lean pork, such as fillet, or skinned, boneless chicken breasts, instead of the steak. For a vegetarian version, use cubed, smoked tofu.

SWEET-&-SOUR SPARERIBS

INGREDIENTS　　　　　　　　　　Serves 4

3½ lbs. pork spareribs
4 tbsp. honey
1 tbsp. Worcestershire sauce
1 tsp. Chinese five spice
　powder
4 tbsp. soy sauce
2½ tbsp. dry sherry

1 tsp. chili sauce
2 garlic cloves, peeled and
　chopped
1½ tbsp. tomato paste
1 tsp. dry mustard powder
　(optional)
scallion curls, to garnish

1 Preheat the oven to 400° F. If necessary, place the ribs on a chopping board, and, using a sharp knife, cut between the ribs to separate them. Place the ribs in a shallow dish in a single layer.

2 Spoon the honey, Worcestershire sauce, Chinese five spice powder, soy sauce, sherry, and chili sauce into a small saucepan, and heat gently, stirring until smooth. Stir in the chopped garlic, tomato paste, and mustard powder, if desired.

3 Pour the honey mixture over the ribs, and spoon over until all the ribs are coated evenly. Cover with plastic wrap and leave to marinate overnight in the refrigerator, occasionally spooning the marinade over the ribs.

4 When ready to cook, remove the ribs from the marinade and place in a shallow roasting pan. Spoon over a little of the marinade, and set aside the remainder. Place the spareribs in the preheated oven, and cook for 35–40 minutes or until cooked and the outsides are crisp. Baste occasionally with the marinade during cooking. Garnish with a few scallion curls, and serve immediately, either as a starter or a side dish.

TASTY TIP

Marinating spareribs overnight not only flavors the meat, but makes it wonderfully tender as well. If you do not have enough time for this, place the ribs in a saucepan and pour in enough water just to cover them. Add 1 tablespoon of wine vinegar, bring to a boil, then simmer gently for 15 minutes. Drain well, toss in the marinade, and roast right away, basting occasionally as before.

LAMB WITH STIR-FRIED VEGETABLES

INGREDIENTS   Serves 4

1¼ lb. lamb fillet, cut into strips
1-in. piece ginger, peeled and
  thinly sliced
2 garlic cloves, peeled and
  chopped
4 tbsp. soy sauce
2 tbsp. dry sherry
2 tsp. cornstarch
4 tbsp. peanut oil
½ cup trimmed and halved
  green beans
2 medium carrots, peeled and
  thinly sliced

1 red bell pepper, deseeded
  and cut into chunks
1 yellow bell pepper, deseeded
  and cut into chunks
8-oz. can water chestnuts,
  drained and halved
3 tomatoes, chopped
freshly cooked sticky rice in
  banana leaves, to serve
  (optional)

1 Place the lamb strips in a shallow dish. Mix together the ginger and half the garlic in a small bowl. Pour over the soy sauce and sherry, and stir well. Pour over the lamb, and stir until coated lightly. Cover with plastic wrap, and leave to marinate for at least 30 minutes, occasionally spooning the marinade over the lamb.

2 Using a slotted spoon, lift the lamb from the marinade and place on a plate. Blend the cornstarch and the marinade together until smooth, and set aside.

3 Heat a wok or large skillet, add 2 tablespoons of the oil, and, when hot, add the remaining garlic, green beans, carrots, and bell peppers, and stir-fry for 5 minutes. Using a slotted spoon, transfer the vegetables to a plate, and keep warm.

4 Heat the remaining oil in the wok, add the lamb, and stir-fry for 2 minutes or until tender. Return the vegetables to the wok with the water chestnuts, tomatoes, and marinade mixture. Bring to a boil, then simmer for 1 minute. Serve immediately, with freshly cooked sticky rice in banana leaves, if desired.

FOOD FACT

Sticky or glutinous rice has a high starch content. The grains stick together when cooked, making it easy to eat with chopsticks.

SZECHUAN BEEF

INGREDIENTS   Serves 4

1 lb. beef tenderloin
3 tbsp. hoisin sauce
2 tbsp. yellow bean sauce
2 tbsp. dry sherry
1 tbsp. brandy
2 tbsp. peanut oil
2 red chilies, deseeded and
   sliced
8 bunches scallions, trimmed
   and chopped
2 garlic cloves, peeled and
   chopped
1-in. piece ginger, peeled and
   thinly sliced

1 carrot, peeled, sliced
   lengthwise, and cut into
   short lengths
2 green bell peppers, deseeded
   and cut into 1-in. pieces
8-oz. can water chestnuts,
   drained and halved
sprigs of cilantro, to garnish
freshly cooked noodles with
   freshly ground Szechuan
   peppercorns, to serve

1 Trim the beef, discarding any sinew or fat, then cut into ¼-in. strips. Place in a large, shallow dish. In a bowl, stir the hoisin sauce, yellow bean sauce, sherry, and brandy together until well blended. Pour over the beef and turn until coated evenly. Cover with plastic wrap and leave to marinate for at least 30 minutes.

2 Heat a wok or large skillet, add the oil and, when hot, add the chilies, scallions, garlic, and ginger, and stir-fry for 2 minutes or until softened. Using a slotted spoon, transfer to a plate and keep warm.

3 Add the carrot and bell peppers to the wok, and stir-fry for 4 minutes or until slightly softened. Transfer to a plate and keep warm.

4 Drain the beef, setting aside the marinade, add to the wok, and stir-fry for 3–5 minutes or until browned. Return the chili mixture, carrot and pepper mixture, and the marinade to the wok, add the water chestnuts, and stir-fry for 2 minutes or until heated through. Garnish with sprigs of cilantro, and serve immediately with the noodles.

FOOD FACT

Water chestnuts grow on a reed-like plant. When peeled, they are white, sweet, and crunchy, and it is their texture, rather than flavor, that makes them such a popular addition to stir-fries.

Cashew & Pork Stir-Fry

INGREDIENTS   Serves 4

1 lb. pork tenderloin
4 tbsp. soy sauce
1 tbsp. cornstarch
1 cup unsalted cashews
4 tbsp. sunflower oil
1 lb. leeks, trimmed and
    shredded
1-in. piece fresh root ginger,
    peeled and thinly sliced
2 garlic cloves, peeled and
    chopped

1 red bell pepper, deseeded
    and sliced
1¼ cups chicken stock
2 tbsp. freshly chopped
    cilantro
freshly cooked noodles, to
    serve

1 Using a sharp knife, trim the pork, discarding any sinew or fat. Cut into ¾-in. slices, and place in a shallow dish. Blend the soy sauce and cornstarch together until smooth and free from lumps, then pour over the pork. Stir until coated in the cornstarch mixture, then cover with plastic wrap, and leave to marinate in the refrigerator for at least 30 minutes.

2 Heat a nonstick skillet until hot, add the cashews, and fry for 2–3 minutes or until toasted, stirring frequently. Transfer to a plate and set aside.

3 Heat a wok or large skillet, add 2 tablespoons of the oil, and, when hot, add the leeks, ginger, garlic, and bell pepper, and stir-fry for 5 minutes or until softened. Using a slotted spoon, transfer to a plate and keep warm.

4 Drain the pork, setting aside the marinade. Add the remaining oil to the wok and, when hot, add the pork and stir-fry for 5 minutes or until browned. Return the vegetables to the wok with the marinade and the stock. Bring to a boil, then simmer for 2 minutes or until the sauce has thickened. Stir in the toasted cashew nuts and chopped cilantro, and serve immediately with freshly cooked noodles.

FOOD FACT

Now grown throughout the tropics, cashews originated in South America. The fruit is large and shiny, and pink, red, or yellow in color. It is sometimes made into a drink or jam. The small, hard-shelled, kidney-shaped seed in the center of the fruit contains the cashew nut.

LAMB MEATBALLS WITH SAVOY CABBAGE

INGREDIENTS

Serves 4

1 lb. fresh ground lamb
1 tbsp. freshly chopped parsley
1 tbsp. freshly shredded ginger
1 tbsp. light soy sauce
1 medium egg yolk
4 tbsp. dark soy sauce
2 tbsp. dry sherry
1 tbsp. cornstarch
3 tbsp. vegetable oil

2 garlic cloves, peeled and chopped
1 bunch scallions, trimmed and shredded
½ savoy cabbage, trimmed and shredded
½ head Chinese cabbage, trimmed and shredded
freshly chopped red chili, to garnish

1 Place the ground lamb in a large bowl with the parsley, ginger, light soy sauce, and egg yolk, and mix together. Divide the mixture into walnut-size pieces, and, using your hands, roll into balls. Place on a baking sheet, cover with plastic wrap, and chill in the refrigerator for at least 30 minutes.

2 Meanwhile, blend together the dark soy sauce, sherry, and cornstarch with 2 tablespoons of cold water in a small bowl until smooth. Set aside until needed.

3 Heat a wok, add the oil, and, when hot, add the meatballs, and cook for 5–8 minutes or until browned all over, turning occasionally. Using a slotted spoon, transfer the meatballs to a large plate, and keep warm.

4 Add the garlic, scallions, Savoy cabbage, and the Chinese cabbage to the wok, and stir-fry for 3 minutes. Add the soy sauce mixture, bring to a boil, then simmer for 30 seconds or until thickened. Return the meatballs to the wok and mix in. Garnish with chopped red chili, and serve immediately.

TASTY TIP

This dish is made with simple, basic ingredients, but you can substitute more Chinese ingredients if you prefer, such as rice wine vinegar instead of sherry, and bok choy leaves instead of savoy cabbage. As the meatballs contain eggs, make sure that they are cooked thoroughly.

BARBECUED PORK FILLET

INGREDIENTS   Serves 4

2 tbsp. honey
2 tbsp. hoisin sauce
2 tsp. tomato paste
1-in. piece ginger, peeled and chopped
1 lb. pork tenderloin
3 tbsp. vegetable oil
1 garlic clove, peeled and chopped
1 bunch scallions, trimmed and chopped

1 red bell pepper, deseeded and cut into chunks
1 yellow bell pepper, deseeded and cut into chunks
2 cups cooked long-grain rice
⅔ cup frozen peas, thawed
2 tbsp. light soy sauce
1 tbsp. sesame oil
½ cup toasted, flaked almonds

1 Preheat the oven to 400° F. Mix together the honey, hoisin sauce, tomato paste, and ginger in a bowl. Trim the pork, discarding any sinew or fat. Place in a shallow dish, and spread the honey and hoisin sauce over the pork to cover completely. Cover with plastic wrap and chill in the refrigerator for 4 hours, turning occasionally.

2 Remove the pork from the marinade, and place in a roasting pan, setting aside the marinade. Cook in the preheated oven for 20–25 minutes or until the pork is tender, and the juices run clear when the meat is pierced with a skewer. Baste occasionally with the marinade during cooking. Remove the pork from the oven, let rest for 5 minutes, then slice thinly, and keep warm.

3 Meanwhile, heat a wok or large skillet, add the vegetable oil, and, when hot, add the garlic, scallions, and bell peppers, and stir-fry for 4 minutes or until softened. Add the rice and peas, and stir-fry for 2 minutes.

4 Add the soy sauce, sesame oil, and flaked almonds, and stir-fry for 30 seconds or until heated through. Tip into a warmed serving dish, and top with the sliced pork. Serve immediately.

HELPFUL HINT

If you have untoasted, flaked almonds, place them on a cookie sheet in the oven for 5–10 minutes while you cook the pork. Check them frequently as nuts burn very easily.

SPICY LAMB & PEPPERS

INGREDIENTS

Serves 4

1¼ lbs. lamb fillet

4 tbsp. soy sauce

1 tbsp. dry sherry

1 tbsp. cornstarch

3 tbsp. vegetable oil

1 bunch scallions, shredded

2 cups broccoli florets

2 garlic cloves, peeled and chopped

1-in. piece ginger, peeled and thinly sliced

1 red bell pepper, deseeded and cut into chunks

1 green bell pepper, deseeded and cut into chunks

2 tsp. Chinese five spice powder

1–2 tsp. dried, crushed chilies, or to taste

1 tbsp. tomato paste

1 tbsp. rice wine vinegar

1 tbsp. brown sugar

freshly cooked noodles, to serve

1 Cut the lamb into ¾-in. slices, then place in a shallow dish. Blend the soy sauce, sherry, and cornstarch together in a small bowl, and pour over the lamb. Turn the lamb until coated lightly with the marinade. Cover with plastic wrap and let marinate in the refrigerator for at least 30 minutes, turning occasionally.

2 Heat a wok or large skillet, add the oil, and, when hot, stir-fry the scallions and broccoli for 2 minutes. Add the garlic, ginger, and bell peppers, and stir-fry for an additional 2 minutes. Using a slotted spoon, transfer the vegetables to a plate and keep warm.

3 Using a slotted spoon, lift the lamb from the marinade, shaking off any excess marinade. Add to the wok and stir-fry for 5 minutes or until browned all over. Set aside the marinade.

4 Return the vegetables to the wok and stir in the Chinese five spice powder, chilies, tomato paste, marinade, vinegar, and sugar. Bring to a boil, stirring constantly, until thickened. Simmer for 2 minutes or until heated through. Serve immediately with noodles.

FOOD FACT

Chinese rice wine, or *shaoxing*, is used for both drinking and cooking, and is an essential ingredient in banquet dishes. If it is unavailable, substitute dry sherry.

BRANDIED LAMB CHOPS

INGREDIENTS   Serves 4

8 lamb chops
3 tbsp. peanut oil
2-in. piece ginger, peeled and
 thinly sliced
2 garlic cloves, peeled and
 chopped
½ lb. button mushrooms,
 wiped and halved if large
2 tbsp. light soy sauce
2 tbsp. dry sherry
1 tbsp. brandy

1 tsp. Chinese five spice
 powder
1 tsp. brown sugar
¾ cup lamb or chicken stock
1 tsp. sesame oil

TO SERVE:
freshly cooked rice
freshly stir-fried vegetables

1 Using a sharp knife, trim the lamb chops, discarding any sinew or fat. Heat a wok or large skillet, add the oil, and, when hot, add the lamb chops and cook for 3 minutes on each side or until browned. Using a fish slice, transfer the lamb chops to a plate, and keep warm.

2 Add the ginger, garlic, and button mushrooms to the wok, and stir-fry for 3 minutes or until the mushrooms have browned.

3 Return the lamb chops to the wok, along with the soy sauce, sherry, brandy, five spice powder, and sugar. Pour in the stock, bring to a boil, then reduce the heat slightly, and simmer for 4–5 minutes or until the lamb is tender, ensuring that the liquid does not evaporate completely. Add the sesame oil, and heat for an additional 30 seconds. Turn into a warmed serving dish, and serve immediately with freshly cooked rice and stir-fried vegetables.

FOOD FACT

Lamb is not widely eaten in China, but Chinese Muslims (who are forbidden to eat pork) often cook it, as do Mongols and people from Sinkiang. Use a good-quality stock for this dish, preferably one without too much salt, as the sauce is reduced slightly. Choose either homemade stock or store-bought fresh stock.

PORK CABBAGE POCKETS

INGREDIENTS   Serves 4

8 large, green cabbage leaves
1 tbsp. vegetable oil
2 celery sticks, trimmed and
  chopped
1 carrot, peeled and thinly
  slice
¼ lb. fresh ground pork
button mushrooms, wiped
  and sliced
1 tsp. Chinese five spice
  powder
⅓ cup cooked long-grain rice

juice of 1 lemon
1 tbsp. soy sauce
⅔ cup chicken stock

FOR THE TOMATO SAUCE:
1 tbsp. vegetable oil
1 bunch scallions, trimmed
  and chopped
14-oz. can chopped tomatoes
1 tbsp. light soy sauce
1 tbsp. freshly chopped mint
freshly ground black pepper

1 Preheat the oven to 350° F. To make the sauce, heat the oil in a heavy-based saucepan, add the scallions, and cook for 2 minutes or until softened.

2 Add the tomatoes, soy sauce, and mint to the saucepan, bring to a boil, cover, then simmer for 10 minutes. Season to taste with pepper. Reheat when needed.

3 Meanwhile, blanch the cabbage leaves in a large saucepan of lightly salted water for 3 minutes. Drain under cold running water. Pat dry with paper towels, and set aside.

4 Heat the oil in a small saucepan, add the celery, carrot, and ground pork, and cook for 3 minutes. Add the mushrooms and cook for 3 minutes. Stir in

the Chinese five spice powder, rice, lemon juice, and soy sauce, and heat through.

5 Place some of the filling in the center of each cabbage leaf, and fold to enclose the filling. Place in a shallow ovenproof dish seam-side down. Pour over the stock, and cook in the preheated oven for 30 minutes. Serve immediately with the reheated tomato sauce.

HELPFUL HINT

Use large, evenly sized leaves, such as savoy cabbage, which become flexible when blanched. If necessary, remove the thicker end of the stalk after blanching.

DUCK IN BLACK BEAN SAUCE

INGREDIENTS   Serves 4

1 lb. duck breast, skinned
1 tbsp. light soy sauce
1 tbsp. Chinese rice wine or
   dry sherry
1 in. piece ginger
3 garlic cloves
2 scallions

2 tbsp. Chinese preserved
   black beans
1 tbsp. peanut or vegetable oil
⅔ cup chicken stock
shredded scallions, to garnish
freshly cooked noodles, to serve

1 Using a sharp knife, trim the duck breasts, removing any fat. Slice thickly and place in a shallow dish. Mix together the soy sauce and Chinese rice wine or sherry, and pour over the duck. Leave to marinate for 1 hour in the refrigerator, then drain and discard the marinade.

2 Peel the ginger and chop finely. Peel the garlic cloves and either chop finely or crush. Trim the roots from the scallions, discard the outer leaves, and chop. Finely chop the Chinese preserved black beans.

3 Heat a wok or large skillet, add the oil, and, when very hot, add the ginger, garlic, scallions, and black beans, and stir-fry for 30 seconds. Add the drained duck, and stir-fry for 3–5 minutes or until the duck is browned.

4 Add the chicken stock to the wok, bring to a boil, then reduce the heat, and simmer for 5 minutes or until the duck is cooked, and the sauce is reduced and thickened. Remove from the heat. Tip onto a bed of freshly cooked noodles, garnish with scallions, and serve immediately.

HELPFUL HINT

The way in which a dish is presented and garnished is extremely important in both Chinese and Thai cuisines. Fine shreds of colorful vegetables are simple to make. For scallion shreds, cut off most of the white bulb end, and trim the tops. Cut the remaining green part lengthwise into fine shreds. These can be curled by soaking them in ice water for a few minutes.

CHINESE-GLAZED GAME HENS WITH GREEN & BLACK RICE

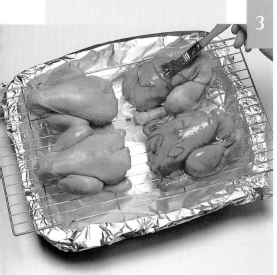

INGREDIENTS

Serves 4

4 oven-ready game hens
salt and freshly ground black
  pepper
1¼ cups apple juice
1 cinnamon stick
2 star anise
½ tsp. Chinese five spice
  powder
⅓ cup dark brown sugar
2 tbsp. ketchup
1 tbsp. cider vinegar

grated zest of 1 orange
2 cups mixed basmati white
  and wild rice
¾ cup snow peas, finely sliced
  lengthwise
1 bunch scallions, trimmed
  and finely shredded
  lengthwise
salt and freshly ground black
  pepper

1 Preheat the oven to 400° F. Rinse the game hens inside and out, and pat dry with paper towels. Using tweezers, remove any feathers. Season well with salt and pepper, then set aside.

2 Pour the apple juice into a small saucepan, and add the cinnamon stick, star anise, and Chinese five spice powder. Bring to a boil, then simmer rapidly until reduced by half. Reduce the heat, stir in the sugar, ketchup, vinegar, and orange zest, and simmer gently until the sugar is dissolved and the glaze is syrupy. Remove from the heat, and let cool completely. Remove the whole spices.

3 Place the game hens on a wire rack set over a pan lined with aluminum foil. Brush generously with the apple glaze.

Roast in the preheated oven for 40–45 minutes or until the juices run clear when the thigh is pierced with a skewer, basting once or twice with the remaining glaze. Remove the game hens from the oven, and let cool slightly.

4 Meanwhile, cook the rice according to the package instructions. Bring a large saucepan of lightly salted water to a boil and add the snow peas. Blanch for 1 minute, then drain thoroughly. As soon as the rice is cooked, drain, and transfer to a warmed bowl. Add the snow peas and scallions, season to taste, and stir well. Arrange on warmed dinner plates, place a game hen on top, and serve immediately.

BRAISED CHICKEN WITH EGGPLANT

INGREDIENTS   Serves 4

3 tbsp. vegetable oil

12 chicken thighs

2 large eggplants, trimmed and cubed

4 garlic cloves, peeled and crushed

2 tsp. freshly shredded ginger

3¾ cups vegetable stock

2 tbsp. light soy sauce

2 tbsp. Chinese preserved black beans

6 scallions, trimmed and thinly sliced diagonally

1 tbsp. cornstarch

1 tbsp. sesame oil

scallion tassels, to garnish

freshly cooked noodles or rice, to serve

1 Heat a wok or large skillet, add the oil, and, when hot, add the chicken thighs and cook over a medium-high heat for 5 minutes or until browned all over. Transfer to a large plate and keep warm.

2 Add the eggplant to the wok, and cook over a high heat for 5 minutes or until browned, turning occasionally. Add the garlic and ginger, and stir-fry for 1 minute.

3 Return the chicken to the wok, pour in the stock, and add the soy sauce and black beans. Bring to a boil, then simmer for 20 minutes or until the chicken is tender. Add the scallions after 10 minutes.

4 Blend the cornstarch with 2 tablespoons of water. Stir into the wok, and simmer until the sauce has thickened. Stir in the sesame oil, heat for 30 seconds, then remove from the heat. Garnish with scallion tassels, and serve immediately with noodles or rice.

TASTY TIP

To make your own Chinese-style vegetable stock, roughly chop 1 onion, 2 celery sticks, and 2 carrots, and place in a large saucepan with a few dried shiitake mushrooms and slices of ginger. Pour in 6 cups cold water, bring to a boil, partially cover, and simmer for about 30 minutes. Let cool, then strain through a fine sieve, discarding the vegetables. Store the stock in the refrigerator.

STIR-FRIED DUCK WITH CASHEWS

INGREDIENTS   Serves 4

1 lb. duck breast, skinned
3 tbsp. peanut or vegetable oil
1 garlic clove, peeled and
  finely chopped
1 tsp. freshly shredded ginger
1 carrot, peeled and sliced
¾ cup trimmed snow peas
2 tsp. Chinese rice wine or dry
  sherry

1 tbsp. light soy sauce
1 tsp. cornstarch
½ cup unsalted cashews, roasted
1 scallion, trimmed and finely
  chopped
1 scallion, shredded
boiled or steamed rice, to serve

1 Trim the duck breasts, discarding any fat, and slice thickly. Heat the wok, add 2 tablespoons of the oil, and, when hot, add the sliced duck breast. Cook for 3–4 minutes or until sealed. Using a slotted spoon, remove from the wok, and let drain on paper towels.

2 Wipe the wok clean and return to the heat. Add the remaining oil, and, when hot, add the garlic and ginger. Stir-fry for 30 seconds, then add the sliced carrots and snow peas. Stir-fry for an additional 2 minutes, then pour in the Chinese rice wine or sherry and soy sauce.

3 Blend the cornstarch with 1 teaspoon of water, and stir into the wok. Mix well and bring to a boil. Return the duck slices to the wok, and simmer for 5 minutes or until the meat and vegetables are tender. Add the cashews, then remove the wok from the heat.

4 Sprinkle with the chopped and shredded scallions, and serve immediately with plain boiled or steamed rice.

HELPFUL HINT

Snow peas are now available year-round. Look for small, bright-green snow peas containing barely formed peas. Store them in the refrigerator for no more than 2 days before using, to maximize their fresh, sweet flavor. To prepare, simply remove the tops and bottoms, pulling away as much string from the edges as you can. Fry the peas in the wok before starting to seal the duck breasts. Make sure the peas do not burn.

STIR-FRIED LEMON CHICKEN

INGREDIENTS

Serves 4

¾ lb. boneless, skinless
  chicken breast
1 large egg white
5 tsp. cornstarch
3 tbsp. vegetable or peanut oil
⅔ cup chicken stock
2 tbsp. fresh lemon juice
2 tbsp. light soy sauce
1 tbsp. Chinese rice wine or
  dry sherry
1 tbsp. sugar

2 garlic cloves, peeled and
  finely chopped
¼ tsp. dried chili flakes, or to
  taste

TO GARNISH:
lemon zest strips
red chili slices

1 Using a sharp knife, trim the chicken, discarding any fat, and cut into thin strips, about 2 in. long and ½ in. wide. Place in a shallow dish. Lightly whisk the egg white and 1 tablespoon of the cornstarch together until smooth. Pour over the chicken strips and mix well until coated evenly. Leave to marinate in the refrigerator for at least 20 minutes.

2 When ready to cook, drain the chicken and set aside. Heat a wok or large skillet, add the oil, and, when hot, add the chicken and stir-fry for 1–2 minutes or until the chicken has turned white. Using a slotted spoon, remove from the wok, and set aside.

3 Wipe the wok clean and return to the heat. Add the chicken stock, lemon juice, soy sauce, Chinese rice wine or sherry,

sugar, garlic, and chili flakes, and bring to a boil. Blend the remaining cornstarch with 1 tablespoon of water, and stir into the stock. Simmer for 1 minute.

4 Return the chicken to the wok, and continue simmering for an additional 2–3 minutes or until the chicken is tender and the sauce has thickened. Garnish with lemon zest strips and red chili slices. Serve immediately.

FOOD FACT

Chili flakes are crushed, dried red chilies and are widely used in parts of China where long strings of red chilies can be seen drying in the sun.

TURKEY & VEGETABLE STIR-FRY

INGREDIENTS   Serves 4

¾ lb. mixed vegetables, such as baby corn, 1 small red bell pepper, bok choy, mushrooms, broccoli florets, and baby carrots
1 red chili
2 tbsp. peanut oil
¾ lb. skinless, boneless turkey breast, sliced into fine strips across the grain
2 garlic cloves, peeled and finely chopped
1-in. piece ginger, peeled and finely shredded

3 scallions, trimmed and finely sliced
2 tbsp. light soy sauce
1 tbsp. Chinese rice wine or dry sherry
2 tbsp. chicken stock or water
1 tsp. cornstarch
1 tsp. sesame oil
freshly cooked noodles or rice, to serve

TO GARNISH:
½ cup toasted cashews
2 scallions, finely shredded
1 cup bean sprouts

1 Slice or chop the vegetables into small pieces, depending on which you use. Halve the baby corn lengthwise, deseed and thinly slice the red bell pepper, tear or shred the bok choy, slice the mushrooms, break the broccoli into small florets, and thinly slice the carrots. Deseed and finely chop the chili.

2 Heat a wok or large skillet, add the oil, and, when hot, add the turkey strips and stir-fry for 1 minute or until they turn white. Add the garlic, ginger, scallions, and chili, and cook for a few seconds.

3 Add the prepared carrot, pepper, broccoli, and mushrooms, and stir-fry for 1 minute. Add the baby corn and bok choy, and stir-fry for 1 minute.

4 Blend the soy sauce, Chinese rice wine or sherry, and stock or water, and pour over the vegetables. Blend the cornstarch with 1 teaspoon of water, and stir into the vegetables, mixing well. Bring to a boil, reduce the heat, then simmer for 1 minute. Stir in the sesame oil. Tip into a warmed serving dish, sprinkle with cashew nuts, shredded scallions, and bean sprouts. Serve immediately with noodles or rice.

FOOD FACT

Bean sprouts are sprouted from mung beans.

CRISPY ROAST DUCK LEGS WITH PANCAKES

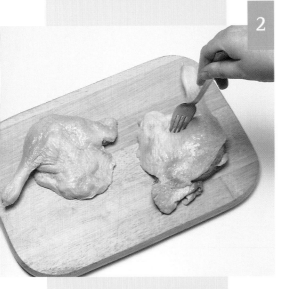

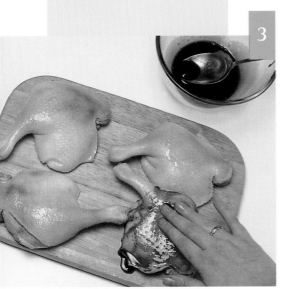

INGREDIENTS   Serves 6

2 lbs. plums, halved

2 tbsp. butter

2 star anise

1 tsp. fresh, finely shredded
 ginger

⅓ cup brown sugar

zest and juice of 1 orange

salt and freshly ground black
 pepper

4 duck legs

3 tbsp. dark soy sauce

2 tbsp. dark brown sugar

½ cucumber, thinly sliced

1 small bunch scallions,
 trimmed and shredded

18 Chinese pancakes, warmed

1 Preheat the oven to 425° F. Pit the plums, and place in a saucepan with the butter, star anise, ginger, brown sugar, and orange zest and juice. Season to taste with pepper. Cook over a gentle heat until the sugar has dissolved. Bring to a boil, then reduce the heat, and simmer for 15 minutes, stirring occasionally, until the plums are soft and the mixture is thick. Remove the star anise and let cool.

2 Using a fork, prick the duck legs all over. Place in a large bowl and pour boiling water over to remove some of the fat. Drain, pat dry on paper towels, and leave until cool.

3 Mix together the soy sauce, dark brown sugar, and ½ teaspoon of salt. Rub this mixture generously over the duck legs. Transfer to a wire rack set over a roasting pan, and roast in the preheated oven for 30–40 minutes or until well cooked and the skin is browned and crisp. Remove from the oven, and let rest for 10 minutes.

4 Shred the duck meat using a fork to hold the hot duck leg and another to remove the meat. Transfer to a warmed serving platter with the cucumber and scallions. Serve immediately with the plum compote and warmed pancakes.

FOOD FACT

Warm pancakes by stacking, wrapping in foil, and placing on a plate in a steamer, or for 15 minutes in the oven, after removing the duck and turning off the oven.

CHINESE BARBECUE-STYLE QUAIL WITH EGGPLANT

INGREDIENTS   Serves 6

4 quail

2 tbsp. salt

3 tbsp. hoisin sauce

1 tbsp. Chinese rice wine or dry sherry

1 tbsp. light soy sauce

1½ lbs. eggplants, trimmed and cubed

1 tbsp. oil

4 garlic cloves, peeled and finely chopped

1 tbsp. freshly chopped ginger

6 scallions, trimmed and finely chopped

3 tbsp. dark soy sauce

¼ tsp. dried chili flakes

1 tbsp. yellow bean sauce

1 tbsp. sugar

TO GARNISH:

sprigs of cilantro

sliced red chili

1 Preheat the oven to 475° F. Rub the quail inside and out with 1 tablespoon of the salt. Mix together the hoisin sauce, Chinese rice wine or sherry, and light soy sauce. Rub the quail inside and out with the sauce. Transfer to a small roasting pan, and roast in the preheated oven for 5 minutes. Reduce the heat to 350° F, and continue to roast for 20 minutes. Turn the oven off, and leave the quail for 5 minutes, then remove and let rest for 10 minutes.

2 Place the eggplant in a colander and sprinkle with the remaining salt. Let drain for 20 minutes, then rinse under cold running water, and pat dry with paper towels.

3 Heat a wok or large skillet over a moderate heat. Add the oil, and, when hot, add the eggplants, garlic, ginger, and 4 of the scallions, and cook for 1 minute. Add the dark soy sauce, chili flakes, yellow bean sauce, sugar, and 2 cups of water. Bring to a boil, then simmer uncovered for 10–15 minutes.

4 Increase the heat to high, and continue to cook, stirring occasionally, until the sauce is reduced and slightly thickened. Spoon the eggplant mixture onto warmed individual plates, and top with the quail. Garnish with the remaining scallions, fresh chili, and cilantro, and serve immediately.

CHINESE BRAISED WHITE CHICKEN WITH THREE SAUCES

INGREDIENTS   Serves 4

3 lb. oven-ready chicken
salt
6 scallions, trimmed
2-in. piece ginger, peeled and
   sliced
2 tsp. Szechuan peppercorns,
   crushed
2½ tsp. sea salt flakes or
   crushed coarse sea salt
2 tsp. freshly shredded ginger
4 tbsp. dark soy sauce
4 tbsp. sunflower oil

1 tsp. superfine sugar
2 garlic cloves, finely chopped
3 tbsp. light soy sauce
1 tbsp. Chinese rice wine or
   dry sherry
1 tsp. sesame oil
3 tbsp. rice vinegar
1 small, hot, red chili,
   deseeded and finely sliced
scallion curls, to garnish
freshly steamed saffron-
   flavored rice, to serve

1 Remove any fat from inside the chicken, rub inside and out with ½ teaspoon of salt, and leave for 20 minutes. Place 3½ quarts water with 2 scallions and the ginger in a saucepan, and bring to a boil. Add the chicken, breast-side down, return to a boil, cover, and simmer for 20 minutes. Remove from the heat, and leave for 1 hour. Remove the chicken, and leave to cool.

2 Fry the Szechuan peppercorns in a nonstick skillet until they darken slightly and smell aromatic. Crush, mix with the sea salt, and set aside.

3 Squeeze the juice from half of the shredded ginger, mix with the dark soy sauce, 1 tablespoon of the sunflower oil, and half the sugar. Set aside.

4 Finely chop the remaining scallions and mix in a bowl with the remaining ginger and garlic. Heat the remaining oil to smoking, and pour over the onion and ginger. When they stop sizzling, stir in the light soy sauce, Chinese rice wine or sherry, and sesame oil. Set aside.

5 Mix together the rice vinegar, remaining sugar, and chili. Stir until the sugar dissolves. Set aside.

6 Remove the skin from the chicken, then remove the legs, and cut them in half at the joint. Lift the breast meat away from the carcass in 2 pieces, and slice thickly crosswise. Sprinkle the pepper and salt mixture over the chicken, garnish with scallion curls, and serve with the dipping sauces, scallion mixture, and rice.

ORANGE-ROASTED WHOLE CHICKEN

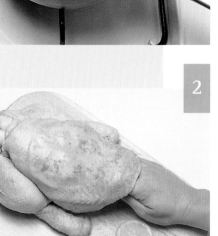

INGREDIENTS   Serves 6

1 small orange, thinly sliced
¼ cup sugar
3 lb. oven-ready chicken
1 small bunch cilantro
1 small bunch fresh mint
2 tbsp. olive oil
1 tsp. Chinese five spice powder
½ tsp. paprika

1 tsp. fennel seeds, crushed
salt and freshly ground black
  pepper
sprigs of cilantro, to garnish
freshly cooked vegetables,
  to serve

1 Preheat the oven to 375° F. Place the orange slices in a small saucepan, cover with water, bring to a boil, then simmer for 2 minutes, and drain. Place the sugar in a clean saucepan with ⅔ cup fresh water. Stir over a low heat until the sugar dissolves, then bring to a boil, add the drained orange slices, and simmer for 10 minutes. Remove from the heat, and leave in the syrup until cold.

2 Remove any excess fat from inside the chicken. Starting at the neck end, carefully loosen the skin of the chicken over the breast and legs without tearing. Push the orange slices, cilantro, and mint under the loosened skin.

3 Mix together the olive oil, Chinese five spice powder, paprika, and crushed fennel seeds, and season to taste with salt and pepper. Brush the chicken skin generously with this mixture. Transfer to a wire rack set over a roasting pan, and roast in the preheated oven for 1½ hours or until the juices run clear when a skewer is inserted into the thickest part of the thigh. Remove from the oven and let rest for 10 minutes. Garnish with sprigs of cilantro, and serve with freshly cooked vegetables.

TASTY TIP

To make oven-baked rice, soften 1 chopped onion in 1 tablespoon sunflower oil in an ovenproof casserole. Stir in 1½ cups long-grain rice, then remove from the heat. Pour in 3¼ cups chicken or vegetable stock, 1 star anise, ½ cinnamon stick, 1 bay leaf, and salt and pepper. Cover and cook for 45 minutes or until tender. Fluff up with a fork and remove the spices.

BAKED THAI CHICKEN WINGS

INGREDIENTS   Serves 4

4 tbsp. honey

1 tbsp. chili sauce

1 garlic clove, peeled and
crushed

1 tsp. freshly shredded ginger

1 lemongrass stalk, finely
chopped, outer leaves
discarded

2 tbsp. lime zest

3–4 tbsp. freshly squeezed
lime juice

1 tbsp. light soy sauce

1 tsp. ground cumin

1 tsp. ground coriander

¼ tsp. ground cinnamon

3 lbs. chicken wings (about 12
large wings)

6 tbsp. mayonnaise

2 tbsp. freshly chopped
cilantro

lemon or lime wedges, to
garnish

1 Preheat the oven to 375° F. In a small saucepan, mix together the honey, chili sauce, garlic, ginger, lemongrass, 1 tablespoon of the lime zest, 2 tablespoons of the lime juice, the soy sauce, cumin, coriander, and cinnamon. Heat gently until just starting to boil, then remove from the heat and let cool.

2 Prepare the chicken wings by folding the tips back under the thickest part of the meat to form a triangle. Arrange in a shallow ovenproof dish. Pour over the honey mixture until well coated. Cover with plastic film, and let marinate in the refrigerator for 4 hours or overnight, turning once or twice.

3 Mix the mayonnaise with the remaining lime zest and juice and the coriander. Set aside to let the flavors develop while the wings are cooking.

4 Arrange the wings on a rack set over a roasting pan lined with aluminum foil. Roast at the top of the preheated oven for 50–60 minutes or until the wings are tender and golden, basting once or twice with the remaining marinade and turning once. Garnish the wings with lemon or lime wedges, and serve immediately with the mayonnaise.

HELPFUL HINT

Alternatively, you could serve a spicy dipping sauce by mixing together 1 tablespoon lime zest and juice with 2 small, fresh, red Thai chilies, deseeded and sliced, 1 tablespoon superfine sugar, 3 tablespoons fish sauce, and 1 tablespoon water.

GRILLED SPICED CHICKEN WITH TOMATO & SHALLOT CHUTNEY

INGREDIENTS   Serves 4

3 tbsp. sunflower oil
2 hot red chilies, deseeded
  and chopped
3 garlic cloves, peeled and
  chopped
1 tsp. ground turmeric
1 tsp. cumin seeds
1 tsp. fennel seeds
1 tbsp. freshly chopped basil
1 tbsp. dark brown sugar
½ cup rice or white wine
  vinegar
2 tsp. sesame oil
4 large chicken breast
  quarters, wings attached

½ lb. small shallots, peeled and
  halved
2 tbsp. Chinese rice wine or
  dry sherry
⅓ cup superfine sugar
½ lb. cherry tomatoes, halved
2 tbsp. light soy sauce

TO GARNISH:
sprigs of cilantro
sprigs of fresh dill
lemon wedges

1 Preheat the broiler to medium. Heat a wok or large skillet, add 1 tablespoon of the sunflower oil, and, when hot, add the chilies, garlic, turmeric, cumin, fennel seeds, and basil. Fry for 5 minutes, add the sugar and 2 tablespoons of vinegar, and stir until the sugar has dissolved. Remove, stir in the sesame oil, and let cool.

2 Make 3 or 4 deep cuts in the thickest part of the chicken breasts. Spread the spice paste over the chicken, place in a dish, cover, and marinate in the refrigerator for at least 4 hours or overnight.

3 Heat the remaining sunflower oil in a saucepan, add the shallots and remaining garlic, and cook gently for 15 minutes. Add the remaining vinegar, Chinese rice wine or sherry, and superfine sugar, along with ¼ cup of water. Bring to a boil, and simmer rapidly for 10 minutes or until thickened. Add the tomatoes with the soy sauce. Simmer for 5–10 minutes or until the liquid is reduced. Let cool.

4 Transfer the chicken pieces to a broiler pan, and cook under the preheated broiler for 15–20 minutes on each side or until the chicken is cooked through, basting frequently. Garnish with cilantro and lemon wedges, and serve immediately with the chutney.

SEARED DUCK WITH PICKLED PLUMS

INGREDIENTS

Serves 4

4 small skinless, boneless
  duck breasts
2 garlic cloves, peeled and
  crushed
1 tsp. hot chili sauce
2 tsp. honey
2 tsp. dark brown sugar
juice of 1 lime
1 tbsp. dark soy sauce
6 large plums, halved and
  pitted

⅓ cup superfine sugar
¼ cup white wine vinegar
¼ tsp. dried chili flakes
¼ tsp. ground cinnamon
1 tbsp. sunflower oil
⅔ cup chicken stock
2 tbsp. oyster sauce
sprigs of fresh Italian parsley,
  to garnish
freshly cooked noodles, to
  serve

1 Make a few deep cuts in each duck breast and place in a shallow dish. Mix together the garlic, chili sauce, honey, brown sugar, lime juice, and soy sauce. Spread over the duck, and leave to marinate in the refrigerator for 4 hours or overnight, if time permits, turning occasionally.

2 Place the plums in a saucepan with the superfine sugar, white wine vinegar, chili flakes, and cinnamon, and bring to a boil. Simmer gently for 5 minutes or until the plums have just softened, then let cool.

3 Remove the duck from the marinade and pat dry with paper towels. Set aside the marinade. Heat a wok or large skillet, add the oil, and, when hot, brown the duck on both sides. Pour in the stock, oyster sauce, and marinade, and simmer for 5 minutes. Remove the duck, and keep warm.

4 Remove the plums from their liquid, and set aside. Pour the liquid into the duck sauce, bring to a boil, then simmer for 5 minutes or until reduced and thickened. Arrange the duck on warmed plates. Divide the plums among the plates, and spoon over the sauce. Garnish with parsley, and serve immediately with noodles.

HELPFUL HINT

When marinating, use a glass or glazed earthenware dish. Plastic dishes will absorb the smell and color of marinades; metal may react with acidic ingredients.

THAI STUFFED OMELETTE

INGREDIENTS Serves 4

1 shallot, peeled and roughly
chopped
1 garlic clove, peeled and
roughly chopped
1 small red chili, deseeded
and roughly chopped
½ cup cilantro leaves
pinch of sugar
2 tsp. light soy sauce
2 tsp. Thai fish sauce
4 tbsp. vegetable or peanut oil
¾ cup skinless, boneless
chicken breast, finely sliced
½ small eggplant, trimmed and
diced
¾ cup wiped and sliced button

or shiitake mushrooms
½ small red bell pepper,
deseeded and sliced
⅓ cup fine green beans,
trimmed and halved
2 scallions, trimmed and
thickly sliced
⅓ cup peas, thawed if frozen
6 medium eggs
salt and freshly ground black
pepper
sprig of fresh basil, to garnish

1 Place the shallot, garlic, chili, cilantro, and sugar in the bowl of a spice grinder or food processor. Blend until finely chopped. Add the soy sauce, fish sauce, and 1 tablespoon of the vegetable oil, and blend briefly to mix into a paste. Set aside.

2 Heat a wok or large skillet, add 1 tablespoon of the oil, and, when hot, add the chicken and eggplant, and stir-fry for 3–4 minutes or until golden. Add the mushrooms, red bell pepper, green beans, and scallions, and stir-fry for 3–4 minutes or until tender, adding the peas for the final minute. Remove from the heat, and stir in the cilantro paste. Set aside.

3 Beat the eggs in a bowl, and season to taste with salt and pepper. Heat the remaining oil in a large nonstick skillet and add the eggs, tilting the pan so that the eggs cover the bottom. Stir the eggs until they are starting to set all over, then cook for 1–2 minutes or until firm and set on the bottom, but still slightly soft on top.

4 Spoon the chicken and vegetable mixture onto half of the omelette, and carefully flip the other half over. Cook over a low heat for 2–3 minutes or until the omelette is set, and the chicken and vegetables are heated through. Garnish with a sprig of basil, and serve immediately.

RED CHICKEN CURRY

INGREDIENTS

Serves 4

1 cup coconut cream
2 tbsp. vegetable oil
2 garlic cloves, peeled and
　finely chopped
2 tbsp. Thai red curry paste
2 tbsp. Thai fish sauce
2 tsp. sugar

1½ cups finely sliced boneless,
　skinless chicken breast
2 cups chicken stock
2 lime leaves, shredded
chopped red chili, to garnish
freshly boiled rice or steamed
　Thai fragrant rice, to serve

1 Pour the coconut cream into a small saucepan and heat gently. Meanwhile, heat a wok or large skillet and add the oil. When the oil is very hot, swirl it around the wok until the wok is lightly coated, then add the garlic and stir-fry for about 10–20 seconds or until the garlic begins to brown. Add the curry paste and stir-fry for a few more seconds, then pour in the warmed coconut cream.

2 Cook the coconut cream mixture for 5 minutes or until the cream has curdled and thickened. Stir in the fish sauce and sugar. Add the finely sliced chicken breast, and cook for 3–4 minutes or until the chicken has turned white.

3 Pour the stock into the wok, bring to a boil, then simmer for 1–2 minutes or until the chicken is cooked through. Stir in the shredded lime leaves. Turn into a warmed serving dish, garnish with chopped red chili, and serve immediately with rice.

TASTY TIP

Thai fragrant rice has a soft, light, fluffy texture. In Thailand it is usually cooked by the following method, starting with cold rather than boiling water to retain its delicate flavor. For 4 people, measure 1¾ cups rice. Rinse under cold running water, then place in a heavy-based saucepan with 2½ cups cold water—the water should come 1 in. above the rice. Add a large pinch of salt, bring to a boil, then simmer for 15 minutes or until most of the water has evaporated. Cover with a tight-fitting lid, turn the heat to the lowest possible setting, and cook for an additional 5 minutes or until all the water has been absorbed and the rice is tender. For added flavor, a light stock can be used instead of the water.

GREEN TURKEY CURRY

INGREDIENTS   Serves 4

4 baby eggplants, trimmed
and quartered

1 tsp. salt

2 tbsp. sunflower oil

4 shallots, peeled and halved,
or quartered if large

2 garlic cloves, peeled and
sliced

2 tbsp. Thai green curry paste

⅔ cup chicken stock

1 tbsp. Thai fish sauce

1 tbsp. lemon juice

1½ cups cubed, boneless,
skinless turkey breast

1 red bell pepper, deseeded
and sliced

¾ cup green beans, trimmed
and halved

⅛ cup creamed coconut

freshly boiled rice or steamed
Thai fragrant rice, to serve

1 Place the eggplants into a colander, and sprinkle with the salt. Set over a plate or in the sink to drain, and leave for 30 minutes. Rinse under cold running water, and pat dry on paper towels.

2 Heat a wok or large skillet, add the sunflower oil, and, when hot, add the shallots and garlic, and stir-fry for 3 minutes or until beginning to brown. Add the curry paste and stir-fry for 1–2 minutes. Pour in the stock, fish sauce, and lemon juice, and simmer for 10 minutes.

3 Add the turkey, red bell pepper, and green beans to the wok with the eggplants. Return to a boil, then simmer for 10–15 minutes or until the turkey and vegetables are tender. Add the creamed coconut, and stir until melted and the sauce

has thickened. Turn into a warmed serving dish, and serve immediately with rice.

FOOD FACT

Several types of eggplant are grown in Thailand. Generally, Thai cooks prefer the small, thin varieties, which have a more delicate flavor. You may find these in Asian markets labeled as "Chinese eggplants," but if you are unable to find them, use baby eggplants, as suggested here.

THAI CHICKEN WITH CHILI & PEANUTS

INGREDIENTS   Serves 4

2 tbsp. vegetable or peanut oil

1 garlic clove, peeled and finely chopped

1 tsp. dried chili flakes

1½ cups finely sliced, boneless, skinless chicken breast

1 tbsp. Thai fish sauce

2 tbsp. peanuts, roasted and roughly chopped

2 cups sugar snap peas

3 tbsp. chicken stock

1 tbsp. light soy sauce

1 tbsp. dark soy sauce

large pinch of sugar

freshly chopped cilantro, to garnish

boiled or steamed rice, to serve

1 Heat a wok or large skillet, add the oil, and, when hot, carefully swirl the oil around the wok until the sides are lightly coated with it. Add the garlic and stir-fry for 10–20 seconds or until starting to brown. Add the chili flakes and stir-fry for a few more seconds.

2 Add the finely sliced chicken to the wok, and stir-fry for 2–3 minutes or until the chicken has turned white.

3 Add the following ingredients, stirring well after each addition: fish sauce, peanuts, sugar snap peas, chicken stock, light and dark soy sauces, and sugar. Give a final stir.

4 Bring the contents of the wok to a boil, then simmer gently for 3–4 minutes or until the chicken and vegetables are tender. Remove from the heat, and tip into a warmed serving dish. Garnish with chopped cilantro, and serve immediately with boiled or steamed rice.

FOOD FACT

Peanut oil is often used in Thai cuisine, because it is mild and almost flavorless, and can be heated to a very high temperature without burning, which makes it perfect for stir-frying and deep-frying. Do not be tempted to stir-fry with olive oil as it does not perform well. Using extra-virgin olive oil would be extremely wasteful, as the delicate flavor of the oil would be destroyed.

THAI STIR-FRIED SPICY TURKEY

INGREDIENTS
Serves 4

2 tbsp. Thai fragrant rice
2 tbsp. lemon juice
3–5 tbsp. chicken stock
2 tbsp. Thai fish sauce
½–1 tsp. cayenne pepper, or to taste
¼ lb. ground raw turkey
2 shallots, peeled and chopped

½ lemongrass stalk, finely sliced, outer leaves discarded
1 lime leaf, finely sliced
1 scallion, trimmed and finely chopped
freshly chopped cilantro, to garnish
Chinese cabbage, to serve

1 Place the rice in a small skillet and cook, stirring constantly, over a medium-high heat for 4–5 minutes or until the rice is browned. Transfer to a spice grinder or blender, and pulse briefly until roughly ground. Set aside.

2 Place the lemon juice, 3 tablespoons of the stock, the fish sauce, and cayenne pepper into a small saucepan, and bring to a boil. Add the ground turkey and return to a boil. Continue cooking over a high heat until the turkey is sealed all over.

3 Add the shallots to the saucepan with the lemongrass, lime leaf, scallion, and rice. Continue cooking for another 1–2 minutes or until the turkey is cooked through, adding a little more stock, if necessary, to keep the mixture moist.

4 Spoon a little of the mixture into each leaf of Chinese cabbage, and arrange on a serving dish or individual plates. Garnish with a little chopped cilantro, and serve immediately.

TASTY TIP

Cooking the rice before grinding gives it a nutty flavor. Take care to cook it only until lightly browned and not at all blackened, as this would spoil the flavor. Chinese cabbage leaves make great serving containers, and enable this dish to be eaten with the fingers. It would also make a delicious starter for 6 to 8 people.

Hot-&-Sour Duck

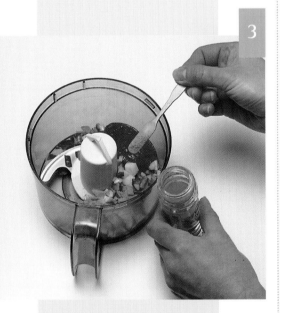

INGREDIENTS   Serves 4

4 small, boneless duck
  breasts, with skin on, thinly
  sliced diagonally
1 tsp. salt
4 tbsp. tamarind pulp
4 shallots, peeled and
  chopped
2 garlic cloves, peeled and
  chopped
1-in. piece ginger, chopped
1 tsp. ground coriander
3 large red chilies, deseeded
  and chopped

½ tsp. turmeric
6 blanched almonds, chopped
½ cup vegetable oil
8-oz. can bamboo shoots,
  drained, rinsed, and finely
  sliced
salt and freshly ground black
  pepper
sprigs of fresh cilantro, to
  garnish
freshly cooked rice, to serve

1 Sprinkle the duck with the salt, cover lightly, and refrigerate for 20 minutes.

2 Meanwhile, place the tamarind pulp in a small bowl, add 4 tablespoons of hot water, and leave for 2–3 minutes or until softened. Press the mixture through a sieve into another bowl to produce about 2 tablespoons of smooth juice.

3 Place the tamarind juice in a food processor with the shallots, garlic, ginger, coriander, chilies, turmeric, and almonds. Blend until smooth, adding a little more hot water if necessary, and set the paste aside.

4 Heat a wok or large skillet, add the oil, and, when hot, stir-fry the duck in batches for about 3 minutes each or until just browned, then drain them on paper towels.

5 Discard all but 2 tablespoons of the oil in the wok. Return to the heat. Add the paste and stir-fry for 5 minutes. Add the duck and stir-fry for 2 minutes. Add the bamboo shoots and stir-fry for 2 minutes. Season to taste with salt and pepper. Turn into a warmed serving dish, garnish with a sprig of cilantro, and serve immediately with rice.

FOOD FACT

Although bamboo shoots are very mild, they add a fresh flavor and some texture to dishes. Occasionally, they can be bought fresh, but the canned version is inexpensive and almost as good.

THAI CHICKEN FRIED RICE

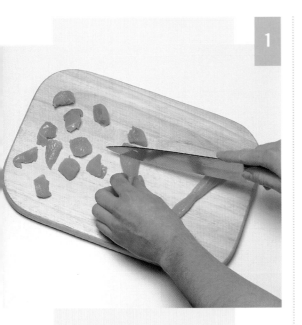

INGREDIENTS   Serves 4

6 oz. boneless chicken breast
2 tbsp. vegetable oil
2 garlic cloves, peeled and
  finely chopped
2 tsp. medium curry paste
3 cups cold cooked rice
1 tbsp. light soy sauce
2 tbsp. Thai fish sauce
large pinch of sugar

freshly ground black pepper

TO GARNISH:
2 scallions, trimmed and
  shredded lengthwise
½ small onion, peeled and very
  finely sliced

1 Using a sharp knife, trim the chicken, discarding any sinew or fat, and cut into small cubes. Set aside.

2 Heat a wok or large skillet, add the oil, and, when hot, add the garlic and cook for 10–20 seconds or until just golden. Add the curry paste and stir-fry for a few seconds. Add the chicken and stir-fry for 3–4 minutes or until tender and the chicken has turned white.

3 Stir the cold cooked rice into the chicken mixture, then add the soy sauce, fish sauce, and sugar, stirring well after each addition. Stir-fry for 2–3 minutes or until the chicken is cooked through, and the rice is piping hot.

4 Check the seasoning and, if necessary, add a little extra soy sauce. Turn the rice and chicken mixture into a warmed serving dish. Season lightly with black pepper, and garnish with shredded scallion and onion slices. Serve immediately.

TASTY TIP

There is a huge range of curry pastes available, from mild and slightly spicy, to burning hot. Although a medium one has been suggested for this dish, you can, of course, use your favorite, but choose a Thai curry paste, such as red or green curry paste, rather than an Indian-style one.

WARM NOODLE SALAD WITH SESAME & PEANUT DRESSING

INGREDIENTS

Serves 4–6

½ cup smooth peanut butter
6 tbsp. sesame oil
3 tbsp. light soy sauce
2 tbsp. red wine vinegar
1 tbsp. freshly shredded ginger
2 tbsp. heavy cream
8-oz. pack Chinese fine egg noodles

2 cups bean sprouts
½ lb. baby corn
1 carrot, peeled and thinly sliced
1 cup snow peas
½ cucumber, cut into thin strips
3 scallions, trimmed and finely shredded

1 Place the peanut butter, 4 tablespoons of the sesame oil, the soy sauce, vinegar, and ginger in a food processor. Blend until smooth, then stir in ⅓ cup hot water, and blend again. Pour in the cream, and blend briefly until smooth. Pour the dressing into a jug and set aside.

2 Bring a saucepan of lightly salted water to a boil, add the noodles and bean sprouts, and cook for 4 minutes or according to the package instructions. Drain, rinse under cold running water, and drain again. Stir in the remaining sesame oil, and keep warm.

3 Bring a saucepan of lightly salted water to a boil, and add the baby corn, carrots, and snow peas, and cook for 3–4 minutes or until just tender but still crisp. Drain and cut the snow peas in half. Slice the baby corn (if very large) into 2–3 pieces, and arrange on a warmed serving dish with the noodles. Add the cucumber strips and scallions. Spoon over a little of the dressing, and serve immediately with the remaining dressing.

FOOD FACT

There are 2 types of sesame oil. The light and pale one is made from untoasted seeds; the other, from toasted seeds, is dark and rich. Its nutty aroma and flavor is overpowering in large quantities, so choose a light version for this recipe. Alternatively, blend 2 tablespoons of toasted sesame oil with 4 tablespoons of a mild oil, such as peanut.

Spicy Cucumber Stir-Fry

INGREDIENTS　　　　　　　　Serves 4

3 tbsp. black soybeans, soaked
　overnight in cold water
1½ cucumbers
2 tsp. salt
1 tbsp. peanut oil
½ tsp. mild chili powder

4 garlic cloves, peeled and
　crushed
5 tbsp. chicken stock
1 tsp. sesame oil
1 tbsp. freshly chopped
　parsley, to garnish

1 Rinse the soaked beans thoroughly, then drain. Place in a saucepan, cover with cold water, and bring to a boil, skimming off any debris that rises to the surface. Boil for 10 minutes, then reduce the heat and simmer for 1–1½ hours. Drain and set aside.

2 Peel the cucumbers, slice lengthwise, and remove the seeds. Cut into 1-in. slices, and place in a colander over a bowl. Sprinkle the salt over the cucumber, and leave for 30 minutes. Rinse thoroughly in cold water, drain, and pat dry with paper towels.

3 Heat a wok or large skillet, add the oil, and, when hot, add the chili powder, garlic, and cooked beans, and stir-fry for 30 seconds. Add the cucumber and stir-fry for 20 seconds.

4 Pour the stock into the wok and cook for 3–4 minutes or until the cucumber is very tender. The liquid will have evaporated at this stage. Remove from the heat and stir in the sesame oil. Turn into a warmed serving dish, garnish with chopped parsley, and serve immediately.

FOOD FACT

Black soybeans are small, oval beans that are referred to as the "meat of the earth" in China, where they were once considered sacred. Soybeans are the only pulse to contain all 8 essential amino acids, so they are an excellent source of protein. They are extremely dense and need to be soaked for at least 5 hours before cooking. Rinse after soaking, place in a saucepan, cover with cold water, and bring to a boil. Boil vigorously for 10 minutes, removing any scum that rises to the surface. Drain, rinse again, then cover with cold water. Bring to a boil, cover, and simmer for 1–1½ hours or until tender.

CHINESE EGG FRIED RICE

INGREDIENTS

Serves 4

1½ cups long-grain rice
1 tbsp. dark sesame oil
2 large eggs
1 tbsp. sunflower oil
2 garlic cloves, peeled and
  crushed
1-in. piece ginger, peeled and
  finely shredded
1 carrot, peeled and thinly
  sliced
1 cup halved snow peas

8-oz. can water chestnuts,
  drained and halved
1 yellow bell pepper, deseeded
  and diced
4 scallions, trimmed and finely
  shredded
2 tbsp. light soy sauce
½ tsp. paprika
salt and freshly ground black
  pepper

1 Bring a saucepan of lightly salted water to a boil, add the rice, and cook for 15 minutes, or according to the package instructions. Drain and let cool.

2 Heat a wok or large skillet, and add the sesame oil. Beat the eggs in a small bowl and pour into the hot wok. Using a fork, draw the egg in from the sides of the pan to the center until it sets, then turn over and cook the other side. When set and golden, turn out onto a board. Leave to cool, then cut into very thin strips.

3 Wipe the wok clean with paper towels, return to the heat, and add the sunflower oil. When hot, add the garlic and ginger, and stir-fry for 30 seconds. Add the remaining vegetables, and continue to stir-fry for 3–4 minutes or until tender but still crisp.

4 Stir the cooked rice into the wok with the soy sauce and paprika, and season to taste with salt and pepper. Fold in the cooked egg strips, and heat through. Tip into a warmed serving dish, and serve immediately.

HELPFUL HINT

Fried rice was originally devised as a tasty way of using leftover rice. The finest is made from recently cooked rice that is cool, but has not been kept in a refrigerator, which means that it is neither too damp nor too dry. Here, the rice is subtly spiced with garlic and ginger. Do not store cooked rice for longer than 24 hours.

VEGETABLE TEMPURA

INGREDIENTS   Serves 4–6

1 cup rice flour
¾ cup all-purpose flour
4 tsp. baking powder
1 tbsp. dried mustard powder
2 tsp. semolina
salt and freshly ground black
  pepper
1¼ cups peanut oil
¼ lb. zucchini, trimmed and
  thickly sliced

¼ lb. snow peas
¼ lb. baby corn
4 small red onions, peeled and
  quartered
1 large red bell pepper,
  deseeded and cut into
  1-in.-wide strips
light soy sauce, to serve

1 Sift the rice flour and the plain flour together in a large bowl, then sift in the baking powder and dried mustard powder.

2 Stir the semolina into the flour mixture, and season to taste with salt and pepper. Gradually beat in 1¼ cups cold water to produce a thin coating batter. Let stand at room temperature for 30 minutes.

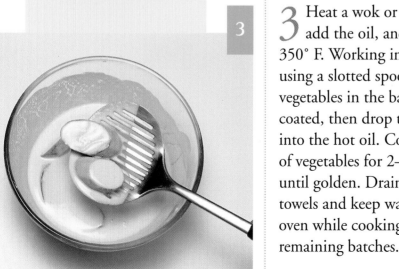

3 Heat a wok or large skillet, add the oil, and heat to 350° F. Working in batches and using a slotted spoon, dip the vegetables in the batter until well coated, then drop them carefully into the hot oil. Cook each batch of vegetables for 2–3 minutes or until golden. Drain on paper towels and keep warm in a low oven while cooking the remaining batches.

4 Transfer the vegetables to a warmed serving platter, and serve immediately with the light soy sauce to use as a dipping sauce.

HELPFUL HINT

The batter for these deep-fried vegetable fritters should be very thin, so that it is transparent when cooked. Take care not to overmix the batter; it should remain slightly lumpy. Deep-fry the vegetables just a few pieces at a time, otherwise the temperature of the oil will drop, and the fritters will not be crisp.

THAI-STYLE CAULIFLOWER & POTATO CURRY

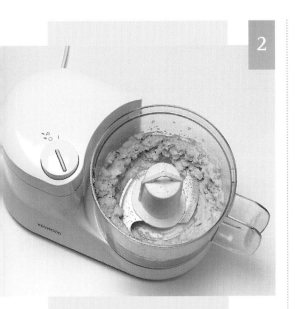

INGREDIENTS

Serves 4

1 lb. new potatoes, peeled and halved or quartered

3 cups cauliflower florets

3 garlic cloves, peeled and crushed

1 onion, peeled and finely chopped

⅓ cup ground almonds

1 tsp. ground coriander

½ tsp. ground cumin

½ tsp. turmeric

3 tbsp. peanut oil

salt and freshly ground black pepper

¼ cup creamed coconut, broken into small pieces

¾ cup vegetable stock

1 tbsp. mango chutney

sprigs of cilantro, to garnish

freshly cooked long-grain rice, to serve

1 Bring a saucepan of lightly salted water to a boil, add the potatoes, and cook for 15 minutes or until just tender. Drain and let cool. Boil the cauliflower for 2 minutes, then drain, and rinse under cold running water. Drain again, and set aside.

2 Meanwhile, blend the garlic, onion, ground almonds, spices, 2 tablespoons of the oil, and salt and pepper in a food processor until a smooth paste is formed. Heat a wok, add the remaining oil, and, when hot, add the spice paste and cook for 3–4 minutes, stirring continuously.

3 Dissolve the creamed coconut in 6 tablespoons of boiling water, and add to the

wok. Pour in the stock, cook for 2–3 minutes, then stir in the cooked potatoes and cauliflower.

4 Stir in the mango chutney, and heat through for 3–4 minutes or until piping hot. Tip into a warmed serving dish, garnish with sprigs of cilantro, and serve immediately with freshly cooked rice.

HELPFUL HINT

Mild flavored vegetables absorb the taste and color of spices in this dish. Take care not to overcook the cauliflower—it should be only just tender for this dish. Broccoli florets would make a good alternative.

Coconut-Baked Zucchini

INGREDIENTS   Serves 4

3 tbsp. peanut oil
1 onion, peeled and finely
   sliced
4 garlic cloves, peeled and
   crushed
½ tsp. chili powder
1 tsp. ground coriander
6–8 tbsp. dried coconut
1 tbsp. tomato paste

1½ lbs. zucchini, thinly sliced
freshly chopped parsley, to
garnish

1 Preheat the oven to 350° F. Lightly grease a large, shallow ovenproof dish. Heat a wok, add the oil, and, when hot, add the onion, and stir-fry for 2–3 minutes or until softened. Add the garlic, chili powder and coriander, and stir-fry for 1–2 minutes.

2 Pour 1¼ cups cold water into the wok, and bring to a boil. Add the dried coconut and tomato paste, and simmer for 3–4 minutes; most of the water will evaporate by this stage. Spoon 4 tablespoons of the spice and coconut mixture into a small bowl, and set aside.

3 Stir the zucchini into the remaining spice and coconut mixture, coating well. Spoon the zucchini into the greased dish, and sprinkle the spice and coconut mixture evenly over the top. Bake uncovered in the preheated oven for 15–20 minutes or until golden. Garnish with chopped parsley, and serve immediately.

HELPFUL HINT

Because coconut is high in fat, dried coconut has a relatively short shelf life and should be stored in a sealed container in a cool, dark cupboard. Warmth, light, and exposure to air all promote rancidity. Unless you use it in large quantities, buy it in small amounts, checking the sell-by date. Once opened, dried coconut should be used within 2 months.

COOKED VEGETABLE SALAD WITH SATAY SAUCE

INGREDIENTS   Serves 4

½ cup peanut oil
1¾ cups unsalted peanuts
1 onion, peeled and finely
  chopped
1 garlic clove, peeled and
  crushed
½ tsp. chili powder
1 tsp. ground coriander
½ tsp. ground cumin
½ tsp. sugar
1 tbsp. dark soy sauce
2 tbsp. fresh lemon juice
2 tbsp. light olive oil
salt and freshly ground black
  pepper

¾ cup green beans, trimmed
  and halved
1 carrot
1 cup cauliflower florets
1 cup broccoli florets
1½ cups trimmed and
  shredded Chinese cabbage
  or bok choy
2 cups bean sprouts
1 tbsp. sesame oil

TO GARNISH:

sprigs of fresh watercress
cucumber, cut into slivers

1 Heat a wok, add the oil, and, when hot, add the peanuts and stir-fry for 3–4 minutes. Drain on paper towels, and let cool. Blend in a food processor to a fine powder.

2 Place the onion, garlic, spices, sugar, soy sauce, lemon juice, and olive oil in a food processor. Season to taste, then process to a paste. Transfer to a wok, and stir-fry for 3–4 minutes.

3 Stir 2½ cups hot water into the paste, and bring to a boil. Add the ground peanuts, and simmer gently for 5–6 minutes or until the mixture thickens. Set aside this satay sauce.

4 Cook the vegetables in batches in lightly salted boiling water, allowing 3–4 minutes for the green beans, carrots, cauliflower, and broccoli, and 2 minutes for the Chinese cabbage and bean sprouts. Drain each batch, drizzle with sesame oil, and arrange on a serving dish. Garnish with watercress and cucumber. Serve with the satay sauce.

FOOD FACT

Peanuts are a member of the pea family, hence their name. They grow underground and are highly nutritious.

MIXED VEGETABLES STIR-FRY

INGREDIENTS

Serves 4

2 tbsp. peanut oil

4 garlic cloves, peeled and finely sliced

1-in. piece ginger, peeled and finely sliced

¾ cup broccoli florets

heaping ½ cup trimmed snow peas

1 carrot, peeled and thinly sliced

1 green bell pepper, deseeded and cut into strips

1 red bell pepper, deseeded and cut into strips

1 tbsp. soy sauce

1 tbsp. hoisin sauce

1 tsp. sugar

salt and freshly ground black pepper

4 scallions, trimmed and shredded, to garnish

1 Heat a wok, add the oil, and, when hot, add the garlic and ginger slices, and stir-fry for 1 minute.

2 Add the broccoli florets to the wok, stir-fry for 1 minute, then add the snow peas, carrots, and the green and red bell peppers, and stir-fry for an additional 3–4 minutes or until tender but still crisp.

3 Blend the soy sauce, hoisin sauce, and sugar in a small bowl. Stir well, season to taste with salt and pepper, and pour into the wok. Transfer the vegetables to a warmed serving dish. Garnish with shredded scallions and serve immediately with a selection of other Thai dishes.

FOOD FACT

Hoisin sauce is a thick, dark brown-red sauce, made by blending soybeans with sugar, vinegar, and spices. It has a spicy, slightly sweet taste and is often used in southern Chinese cooking. It may also be served as a sauce for Bejing duck instead of the more traditional sweet bean sauce.

HELPFUL HINT

Vary the combination of vegetables—try asparagus spears cut into short lengths, sliced mushrooms, green beans, red onion wedges, and cauliflower florets.

THAI STUFFED EGGS WITH SPINACH & SESAME SEEDS

INGREDIENTS   Makes 8

4 large eggs
salt and freshly ground black
    pepper
½ lb. baby spinach
2 garlic cloves, peeled and
    crushed
1 tbsp. scallions, trimmed and
    finely chopped
1 tbsp. sesame seeds

¾ cup all-purpose flour
1 tbsp. light olive oil
1¼ cups vegetable oil for frying

TO GARNISH:
sliced red chili
fresh chives

1 Bring a small saucepan of water to a boil, add the eggs, bring back to a boil, and cook for 6–7 minutes. Plunge into cold water, then peel and cut in half lengthwise. Using a teaspoon, remove the yolks, and place in a bowl. Set aside the whites.

2 Place 1 teaspoon of water and ½ teaspoon of salt in a saucepan, add the spinach, and cook until tender and wilted. Drain, squeeze out the excess moisture, and chop. Mix with the egg yolk, then stir in the garlic, scallions, and sesame seeds. Season to taste with salt and pepper. Fill the egg whites with the mixture, smoothing into a mound.

3 Place the flour in a bowl with the olive oil, a large pinch of salt, and ½ cup warm water. Beat together to make a smooth batter.

4 Heat a wok, add the vegetable oil, and heat to 350° F. Dip the stuffed eggs in the batter, allowing any excess to drip back into the bowl, and deep-fry in batches for 3–4 minutes or until golden brown. Cook the eggs filled-side down first, then turn them over to finish frying. Remove from the wok with a slotted spoon, and drain on paper towels. Serve hot or cold, garnished with chives and chili rings.

HELPFUL HINT

Eggs are often stuffed with a combination of pork and crabmeat, but this vegetarian version makes a delicious alternative. They can be made up to 24 hours before serving.

SAVORY WONTONS

INGREDIENTS

Makes 15

¼ lb. phyllo pastry or wonton squares
15 whole chives
½ lb. spinach
2 tbsp. butter
½ tsp. salt
2 cups wiped and roughly chopped mushrooms
1 garlic clove, peeled and crushed
1–2 tbsp. dark soy sauce
1-in. piece ginger, peeled and finely shredded

salt and freshly ground black pepper
1 small egg, beaten
1¼ cups peanut oil for deep-frying

TO GARNISH:
scallion curls
radish roses

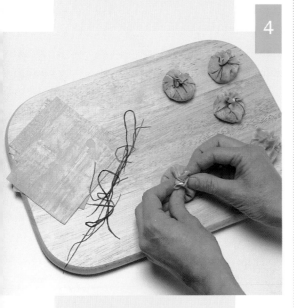

1 Cut the phyllo pastry or wonton skins into 5-in. squares, stack, and cover with plastic wrap. Chill in the refrigerator while preparing the filling. Blanch the chives in boiling water for 1 minute, drain, and set aside.

2 Melt the butter in a saucepan, add the spinach and salt, and cook for 2–3 minutes or until wilted. Add the mushrooms and garlic, and cook for 2–3 minutes or until tender.

3 Transfer the spinach and mushroom mixture to a bowl. Stir in the soy sauce and ginger. Season to taste with salt and pepper.

4 Place a small spoonful of the spinach and mushroom mixture onto a pastry or wonton square, and brush the edges with beaten egg. Gather up the 4 corners to make a little bag and tie with a chive leaf. Fill the remainder of the wontons.

5 Heat a wok, add the oil, and heat to 350° F. Deep-fry the wontons in batches for 2–3 minutes or until golden and crisp. Drain on paper towels, and serve immediately, garnished with scallion curls and radish roses.

HELPFUL HINT

It is important to cover the phyllo pastry or wonton squares with plastic wrap when they are not being filled, to keep them from drying out.

Corn Fritters with Hot & Spicy Relish

INGREDIENTS Makes 16–20

11-oz. can corn, drained
1 onion, peeled and very finely chopped
1 scallion, trimmed and very finely chopped
½ tsp. chili powder
1 tsp. ground coriander
4 tbsp. all-purpose flour
1 tsp. baking powder
1 medium egg
salt and freshly ground black pepper
1¼ cups peanut oil

sprigs of cilantro, to garnish

FOR THE SPICY RELISH:
3 tbsp. sunflower oil
1 onion, peeled and very finely chopped
¼ tsp. dried, crushed chilies
2 garlic cloves, peeled and crushed
2 tbsp. plum sauce

1 Make the relish. Heat a wok, add the sunflower oil, and, when hot, add the onion and stir-fry for 3–4 minutes or until softened. Add the chilies, and garlic, stir-fry for 1 minute, then let cool slightly. Stir in the plum sauce, transfer to a food processor, and blend until the consistency of chutney. Set aside.

2 Place the corn in a food processor and blend briefly until just mashed. Transfer to a bowl with the onions, chili powder, coriander, flour, baking powder, and egg. Season to taste with salt and pepper, and mix together.

3 Heat a wok, add the oil, and heat to 350° F. Working in batches, drop a few spoonfuls of the corn mixture into the oil, and deep-fry for 3–4 minutes or until golden and crispy, turning occasionally. Using a slotted spoon, remove and drain on paper towels. Arrange on a warmed serving platter, garnish with sprigs of cilantro, and serve immediately with the relish.

TASTY TIP

To make this dish the traditional way, brush 2 ears of corn with peanut oil, and grill for 7–8 minutes or until the kernels are beginning to brown. When the ears are cool enough to handle, cut off the kernels.

CHINESE LEAVES WITH SWEET-&-SOUR SAUCE

INGREDIENTS   Serves 4

1 head Chinese cabbage	3 tbsp. orange juice
½ lb. bok choy	2 tbsp. tomato paste
1 tbsp. cornstarch	3 tbsp. sunflower oil
1 tbsp. soy sauce	1 tbsp. butter
2 tbsp. brown sugar	1 tsp. salt
3 tbsp. red wine vinegar	2 tbsp. toasted sesame seeds

1 Discard any tough outer leaves and stalks from the Chinese cabbage and bok choy, and wash well. Drain thoroughly and pat dry with paper towels. Shred the Chinese cabbage and bok choy lengthwise. Set aside.

2 In a small bowl, blend the cornstarch with 4 tablespoons of water. Add the soy sauce, sugar, vinegar, orange juice, and tomato paste, and stir until blended thoroughly.

3 Pour the sauce into a small saucepan, and bring to a boil. Simmer gently for 2–3 minutes or until the sauce is thickened and smooth.

4 Meanwhile, heat a wok or large skillet, and add the sunflower oil and butter. When melted, add the prepared Chinese cabbage and bok choy, sprinkle with the salt, and stir-fry for 2 minutes. Reduce the heat, and cook gently for an additional 1–2 minutes or until tender.

5 Transfer the Chinese cabbage and bok choy to a warmed serving platter, and drizzle with the warm sauce. Sprinkle with the toasted sesame seeds, and serve immediately.

FOOD FACT

Chinese cabbage has a mild, delicate, cabbage-like flavor. It has pale, tightly wrapped, crinkly leaves and crisp white stems. Because it is now grown in several countries worldwide, it is available in stores all year round. They will keep for at least a week in the refrigerator.

BEAN & CASHEW STIR-FRY

INGREDIENTS   Serves 4

3 tbsp. sunflower oil
1 onion, peeled and finely
   chopped
1 celery stalk, trimmed and
   chopped
1-in. piece ginger, peeled and
   grated
2 garlic cloves, peeled and
   crushed
1 red chili, deseeded and
   finely chopped
1 cup trimmed and halved fine
   green beans

1¼ cups snow peas, sliced
   diagonally into thirds
2⅓ cups unsalted cashews
1 tsp. brown sugar
½ cup vegetable stock
2 tbsp. dry sherry
1 tbsp. light soy sauce
1 tsp. red wine vinegar
salt and freshly ground black
   pepper
freshly chopped cilantro, to
   garnish

1 Heat a wok or large skillet, add the oil, and, when hot, add the onion and celery, and stir-fry gently for 3–4 minutes or until softened.

2 Add the ginger, garlic, and chili to the wok, and stir-fry for 30 seconds. Stir in the green beans, snow peas, and cashews, and continue to stir-fry for 1–2 minutes or until the nuts are golden brown.

3 Dissolve the sugar in the stock, then blend with the sherry, soy sauce, and vinegar. Stir into the bean mixture, and bring to a boil. Simmer gently, stirring occasionally, for 3–4 minutes or until the beans and snow peas are tender but still crisp, and the sauce has thickened slightly. Season to taste with salt and pepper. Transfer to a warmed serving bowl, or spoon onto individual plates. Sprinkle with freshly chopped cilantro and serve immediately.

FOOD FACT

Spicy and warm, cilantro features frequently in Thai and some Chinese dishes. It has a similar appearance to Italian parsley, but the flavor is completely different. It is often sold with its roots intact, and these are sometimes used in Thai curry pastes, as they have a far more intense flavor than the leaves.

FRIED RICE WITH BAMBOO SHOOTS & GINGER

INGREDIENTS   Serves 4

4 tbsp. sunflower oil

1 onion, peeled and finely chopped

1⅓ cups long-grain rice

3 garlic cloves, peeled and cut into slivers

1-in. piece ginger, peeled and grated

3 scallions, trimmed and chopped

2 cups vegetable stock

¼ lb. button mushrooms, wiped and halved

½ cup frozen peas, thawed

2 tbsp. light soy sauce

17-oz. can bamboo shoots, drained and thinly sliced

salt and freshly ground black pepper

cayenne pepper, to taste

fresh cilantro, to garnish

1 Heat a wok, add the oil, and, when hot, add the onion and cook gently for 3–4 minutes. Add the rice and cook for 3–4 minutes or until golden, stirring frequently.

2 Add the garlic, ginger, and chopped scallions to the wok, and stir well. Pour the chicken stock into a small saucepan and bring to a boil. Carefully ladle the hot stock into the wok, stir well, then simmer gently for 10 minutes or until most of the liquid has been absorbed.

3 Stir the button mushrooms, peas, and soy sauce into the wok, and continue to cook for an additional 5 minutes or until the rice is tender, adding a little extra stock if necessary.

4 Add the bamboo shoots to the wok and carefully stir in. Season to taste with salt, pepper, and cayenne pepper. Cook for 2–3 minutes or until heated through. Tip onto a warmed serving dish, garnish with cilantro, and serve immediately.

FOOD FACT

Button, cap, and flat mushrooms are the same type of mushroom, but in different stages of maturity. The button mushroom is the youngest, and therefore has the mildest flavor. Brown-capped, chestnut mushrooms, which have a richer, nutty flavor could also be used here.

SPRING ROLLS WITH MIXED VEGETABLES

INGREDIENTS
Makes 12

2 tbsp. sesame oil

1 cup broccoli florets, cut into small pieces

1 carrot, peeled and thinly sliced

1 large zucchini, cut into strips

1 cup finely chopped button mushrooms

1-in. piece ginger, peeled and finely shredded

1 garlic clove, peeled and finely chopped

4 scallions, trimmed and finely chopped

1½ cups bean sprouts

1 tbsp. light soy sauce

pinch of cayenne pepper

4 tbsp. all-purpose flour

12 sheets phyllo pastry

1¼ cups peanut oil

scallion curls, to garnish

1 Heat a wok, add the sesame oil, and, when hot, add the broccoli, carrots, zucchini, mushrooms, ginger, garlic, and scallions, and stir-fry for 1–2 minutes or until slightly softened.

2 Turn into a bowl, add the bean sprouts, soy sauce, and cayenne pepper, and mix together. Transfer the vegetables to a colander, and drain for 5 minutes. Blend the flour with 2–3 tablespoons of water to form a paste, and set aside.

3 Fold a sheet of phyllo pastry in half and in half again, brushing a little water between each layer. Place a spoonful of the drained vegetable mixture on the pastry. Brush a little of the flour paste along the edges. Turn the edges into the center, then roll up and seal. Repeat with the rest.

4 Wipe the wok clean, return to the heat, add the oil, and heat to 375° F. Add the spring rolls in batches, and deep-fry for 2–3 minutes or until golden. Drain on paper towels, arrange on a platter, garnish with scallion curls, and serve immediately.

TASTY TIP

For a lower fat version of this dish, you can bake the spring rolls. Lightly brush them with peanut oil, place on a cookie sheet, and cook on the center shelf of a preheated oven at 375° F for 10 minutes or until golden brown and crisp.

THAI CURRY WITH TOFU

INGREDIENTS   Serves 4

3¼ cups coconut milk

1½ lbs. tofu, drained and cut into small cubes

salt and freshly ground black pepper

4 garlic cloves, peeled and chopped

1 large onion, peeled and cut into wedges

1 tsp. crushed, dried chilies

grated zest of 1 lemon

1-in. piece ginger, peeled and finely shredded

1 tbsp. ground coriander

1 tsp. ground cumin

1 tsp. turmeric

2 tbsp. light soy sauce

1 tsp. cornstarch

Thai fragrant rice, to serve

TO GARNISH:

2 red chilies, deseeded and cut into rings

1 tbsp. freshly chopped cilantro

lemon wedges

1 Pour 2½ cups of the coconut milk into a saucepan, and bring to a boil. Add the tofu, season to taste with salt and pepper, and simmer gently for 10 minutes. Using a slotted spoon, remove the tofu and place on a plate. Set aside the coconut milk.

2 Place the garlic, onion, dried chilies, lemon zest, ginger, spices, and soy sauce in a blender or food processor, and blend until a smooth paste is formed. Pour the remaining ¾ cup coconut milk into a clean saucepan and whisk in the spicy paste. Cook, stirring continuously, for 15 minutes or until the curry sauce is very thick.

3 Gradually whisk the coconut into the curry, and heat to simmering point. Add the cooked tofu and cook for 5–10 minutes. Blend the cornstarch

with 1 tablespoon of cold water and stir into the curry. Cook until thickened. Turn into a warmed serving dish, and garnish with chili, lemon wedges, and cilantro. Serve immediately with Thai fragrant rice.

FOOD FACT

Use firm tofu for this dish, either plain, marinated, or smoked, all available from health-food and Asian markets. Simmer it very gently in the coconut milk, stirring only occasionally so that it does not break up. Firm tofu can be kept in the refrigerator for up to a week in a bowl of water.

CHINESE OMELETTE

INGREDIENTS

Serves 1

1 cup bean sprouts
1 small carrot, peeled and
thinly sliced
½-in. piece ginger, peeled and
finely shredded
1 tsp. soy sauce
2 large eggs
salt and freshly ground black
pepper
1 tbsp. dark sesame oil

TO SERVE:
tossed green salad
Special Fried Rice (see page
114)
soy sauce

1 Lightly rinse the bean sprouts, then place in the top of a bamboo steamer with the carrots. Add the grated ginger and soy sauce. Set the steamer over a pan or wok half-filled with gently simmering water, and steam for 10 minutes or until the vegetables are tender but still crisp. Set aside and keep warm.

2 Whisk the eggs in a bowl until frothy, and season to taste with salt and pepper. Heat an 8-in. omelette pan or skillet, add the sesame oil, and when very hot, pour in the beaten eggs. Whisk the eggs around with a fork, then allow them to cook and start to set. When the surface starts to bubble, lift the edges and tilt the pan to allow the uncooked egg to run underneath.

3 Spoon the bean sprout and carrot mixture over the top of the omelette and allow it to cook a little longer. When it has set, slide the omelette onto a warmed serving dish, and carefully roll up. Serve immediately with a tossed green salad, special fried rice, and extra soy sauce.

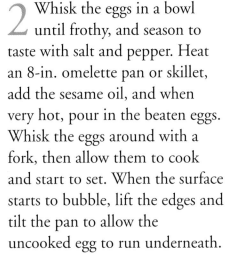

TASTY TIP

Any vegetables work well with this omelette. Try sliced scallions, fine strips of red or green bell peppers, snow peas halved lengthwise, or a few green beans. Cut them into even-size pieces so that they are all tender at the same time.

CRISPY PANCAKE ROLLS

INGREDIENTS

Makes 8

1¼ cups all-purpose flour
pinch of salt
1 medium egg
4 tsp. sunflower oil
2 tbsp. light olive oil
¾-in. piece ginger, peeled and
    finely shredded
1 garlic clove, peeled and
    crushed
½ lb. tofu, drained and diced
2 tbsp. soy sauce

1 tbsp. dry sherry
1½ cups wiped and chopped
    button mushrooms
1 celery stalk, trimmed and
    finely chopped
2 scallions, trimmed and finely
    chopped
2 tbsp. peanut oil
fresh cilantro and sliced
    scallion, to garnish

1 Sift 1 cup of the flour with the salt into a large bowl, make a well in the center, and drop in the egg. Beat to form a smooth, thin batter, gradually adding 1¼ cups of water and drawing in the flour from the sides of the bowl. Mix the remaining flour with 1–2 tablespoons of water to make a thick paste. Set aside.

2 Heat a little sunflower oil in an 8-in. omelette pan or skillet, and pour in 2 tablespoons of the batter. Cook for 1–2 minutes, flip over, and cook for an additional 1–2 minutes or until firm. Slide from the pan and keep warm. Make more pancakes with the remaining batter.

3 Heat a wok or large skillet, add the olive oil, and, when hot, add the ginger, garlic, and tofu, stir-fry for 30 seconds, then pour in the soy sauce and sherry. Add the mushrooms, celery,

and scallions. Stir-fry for 1–2 minutes, then remove from the wok and let cool.

4 Place a little filling in the center of each pancake. Brush the edges with the flour paste, fold in the edges, then roll up into pockets. Heat the peanut oil to 350° F in the wok. Fry the pancake rolls for 2–3 minutes or until golden. Serve immediately, garnished with scallions and cilantro.

HELPFUL HINT

The pancakes can be made a day in advance. Place them on a plate interleaving with paper towels. Cover with plastic wrap and keep in the refrigerator. Bring to room temperature for 30 minutes before frying.

VEGETABLES IN COCONUT MILK WITH RICE NOODLES

INGREDIENTS   Serves 4

⅓ cup creamed coconut

1 tsp. salt

2 tbsp. sunflower oil

2 garlic cloves, peeled and
  finely chopped

2 red bell peppers, deseeded
  and cut into thin strips

1-in. piece of ginger, peeled
  and cut into thin strips

¼ lb. baby corn

2 tsp. cornstarch

2 avocados, medium-ripe but
  firm

1 small head Romaine lettuce,
  cut into thick strips

freshly cooked rice noodles, to
  serve

1 Roughly chop the creamed coconut, place in a bowl with the salt, then pour in 2½ cups of boiling water. Stir until the coconut has dissolved completely, and set aside.

2 Heat a wok or large skillet, add the oil, and, when hot, add the chopped garlic, sliced bell peppers, and ginger. Cook for 30 seconds, then cover and cook very gently for 10 minutes or until the peppers are soft.

3 Pour in the coconut milk and bring to a boil. Stir in the baby corn, cover, and simmer for 5 minutes. Blend the cornstarch with 2 teaspoons of water, pour into the wok, and cook, stirring, for 2 minutes or until thickened slightly.

4 Cut the avocados in half, peel, pit, and slice. Add to the wok with the lettuce strips, and stir until well mixed and heated through. Serve immediately on a bed of rice noodles.

FOOD FACT

Dried, flat rice noodles, rice sticks, and stir-fry rice noodles are all made from rice flour. They come in varying thicknesses. Check on the package for the cooking instructions; they usually need to be soaked in boiling water for about 2–3 minutes, or slightly longer in hot water.

THAI FRIED NOODLES

INGREDIENTS   Serves 4

1 lb. tofu
2 tbsp. dry sherry
4 oz. medium egg noodles
¾ cup snow peas, halved
3 tbsp. peanut oil
1 onion, peeled and finely
  sliced
1 garlic clove, peeled and
  finely sliced
1-in. piece fresh root ginger,
  peeled and finely sliced
2 cups bean sprouts
1 tbsp. Thai fish sauce

2 tbsp. light soy sauce
½ tsp. sugar
salt and freshly ground black
  pepper
½ zucchini, thinly sliced

TO GARNISH:
2 tbsp. roasted peanuts,
  roughly chopped
sprigs of fresh basil

1 Cut the tofu into cubes and place in a bowl. Sprinkle with the sherry, and toss to coat. Cover loosely, and let marinate in the refrigerator for 30 minutes.

2 Bring a large saucepan of lightly salted water to a boil, and add the noodles and snow peas. Simmer for 3 minutes, or according to the package instructions, then drain, and rinse under cold, running water. Leave to drain again.

3 Heat a wok or large skillet, add the oil, and, when hot, add the onion and stir-fry for 2–3 minutes. Add the garlic and ginger, and stir-fry for 30 seconds. Add the bean sprouts and tofu, then stir in the Thai fish sauce, soy sauce, and sugar, and season to taste.

4 Stir-fry the tofu mixture over a medium heat for 2–3 minutes, then add the zucchini, noodles, and snow peas, and stir-fry for an additional 1–2 minutes. Tip into a warmed serving dish, or spoon onto individual plates. Sprinkle with the peanuts, add a sprig of basil, and serve immediately.

FOOD FACT

Tofu is very bland, and it readily absorbs the flavors of other ingredients. It can be marinated in mild or strong ingredients, as desired. Here it is gently tossed in sherry and then added toward the end of cooking to retain the maximum amount of flavor.

CHICKEN & LAMB SATAY

INGREDIENTS

Makes 16

½ lb. skinless, boneless
  chicken
½ lb. lean, boneless lamb

FOR THE MARINADE:
1 small onion, peeled and
  finely chopped
2 garlic cloves, peeled and
  crushed
1-in. piece fresh ginger, peeled
  and finely shredded
4 tbsp. soy sauce
1 tsp. ground coriander
2 tsp. dark brown sugar
2 tbsp. lime juice
1 tbsp. vegetable oil

FOR THE PEANUT SAUCE:
1¼ cups coconut milk
4 tbsp. crunchy peanut butter
1 tbsp. Thai fish sauce
1 tsp. lime juice
1 tbsp. chili powder
1 tbsp. brown sugar
salt and freshly ground black
  pepper

TO GARNISH:
sprigs of fresh cilantro
lime wedges

1 Soak the bamboo skewers for 30 minutes. Preheat the barbecue or broiler just before cooking. Cut the chicken and lamb into thin strips, about 3 in. long, and place in 2 shallow dishes. Blend all the marinade ingredients together, then pour half over the chicken and half over the lamb. Stir until lightly coated, then cover with plastic wrap and marinate in the refrigerator for at least 2 hours, turning occasionally.

2 Remove the chicken and lamb from the marinade, and thread onto the skewers. Set aside the marinade. Cook on the barbecue or broiler for 8–10 minutes or until cooked, turning and brushing with the marinade.

3 Meanwhile, make the peanut sauce. Blend the coconut milk with the peanut butter, fish sauce, lime juice, chili powder, and sugar. Pour into a saucepan, and cook gently for 5 minutes, stirring occasionally, then season to taste with salt and pepper. Garnish with cilantro and lime wedges, and serve the satay with the prepared sauce.

HELPFUL HINT

You can use metal skewers for this dish, but bamboo ones are more traditional, and they are inexpensive. Soaking them in cold water prevents them from scorching during cooking.

CORN CAKES

INGREDIENTS

Serves 6–8

2¼ cups self-rising flour
3 tbsp. Thai red curry paste
2 tbsp. light soy sauce
2 tsp. sugar
2 kaffir lime leaves, finely
   shredded
12 fine green beans, trimmed,
   finely chopped, and
   blanched
12-oz. can corn, drained
salt and freshly ground black
   pepper
2 medium eggs

1 cup fresh white bread
   crumbs
vegetable oil for deep-frying

FOR THE DIPPING SAUCE:
2 tbsp. hoisin sauce
1 tbsp. light brown sugar
1 tbsp. sesame oil

TO SERVE:
cucumber slices
scallions, sliced diagonally

1 Place the flour in a bowl, make a well in the center, then add the curry paste, soy sauce, sugar, shredded kaffir lime leaves, green beans, and corn. Season to taste with salt and pepper, then beat 1 of the eggs and add to the mixture. Stir in with a fork, adding 1–2 tablespoons of cold water to form a stiff dough. Knead lightly on a floured surface, and form into a ball.

2 Divide the mixture into 16 pieces, and shape into small balls, then flatten to form cakes about ½ in. thick and 3 in. in diameter. Beat the remaining egg, and pour into a shallow dish. Dip the cakes first in a little beaten egg, then in the bread crumbs until lightly coated.

3 Heat the oil in either a wok or deep-fat fryer to 350° F, and deep-fry the cakes for 2–3 minutes or until golden brown in color. Using a slotted spoon, remove and drain on paper towels.

4 Meanwhile, blend the hoisin sauce, sugar, 1 tablespoon of water, and the sesame oil together until smooth, and pour into a small bowl. Serve immediately with the corn cakes, cucumber, and scallions.

HELPFUL HINT

If you cannot get lime leaves, use 2 teaspoons of finely grated lime or lemon zest instead.

SOUR-&-SPICY SHRIMP SOUP

INGREDIENTS   Serves 4

2 oz. rice noodles
1 cup Chinese dried
   mushrooms
4 scallions, trimmed
2 small green chilies
3 tbsp. freshly chopped
   cilantro
2½ cups chicken stock
1-in. piece ginger, peeled and
   finely shredded

2 lemongrass stalks, finely
   chopped, outer leaves
   discarded
4 kaffir lime leaves
12 raw jumbo shrimp, peeled,
   with tails left on
2 tbsp. Thai fish sauce
2 tbsp. lime juice
salt and freshly ground black
   pepper

1 Place the noodles in cold water and let soak while preparing the soup. Place the dried mushrooms in a small bowl, cover with almost-boiling water, and leave for 20–30 minutes. Drain, strain, and set aside the soaking liquid. Cut off and discard any woody stems from the mushrooms.

2 Finely shred the scallions and place in a small bowl. Cover with ice-cold water and refrigerate until the scallions have curled.

3 Place the green chilies and 2 tablespoons of the chopped cilantro in a mortar and pestle and pound to a paste. Set aside.

4 Pour the stock into a saucepan, and bring gently to a boil. Stir in the ginger, lemongrass, and lime leaves, with the mushrooms and their liquid. Return to a boil.

5 Drain the noodles, add to the soup with the shrimp, Thai fish sauce, and lime juice, and then stir in the chili and cilantro paste. Bring to a boil, then simmer for 3 minutes. Stir in the remaining chopped cilantro, and season to taste with salt and pepper. Ladle into warmed bowls, sprinkle with the scallion curls, and serve immediately.

HELPFUL HINT

You will need about ⅔ cup of almost-boiling water to cover the Chinese dried mushrooms. After soaking the mushrooms, rinse them under cold running water to remove any traces of grit. Also strain the soaking liquid through a very fine sieve or a piece of cheesecloth before adding to the stock.

DIM SUM PORK POCKETS

INGREDIENTS
Makes about 40

½ cup canned water chestnuts, drained and finely chopped

¾ cup raw shrimp, peeled, deveined, and coarsely chopped

12 oz. ground pork

2 tbsp. smoked bacon, finely chopped

1 tbsp. light soy sauce, plus extra to serve

1 tsp. dark soy sauce

1 tbsp. Chinese rice wine

2 tbsp. ginger, peeled and finely chopped

3 scallions, trimmed and finely chopped

2 tsp. sesame oil

1 medium egg white, lightly beaten

salt and freshly ground black pepper

2 tsp. sugar

40 wonton squares, thawed if frozen

toasted sesame seeds, to garnish

soy sauce, to serve

1 Place the water chestnuts, shrimp, pork, and bacon in a bowl, and mix together. Add the soy sauces, Chinese rice wine, ginger, chopped scallions, sesame oil, and egg white. Season to taste with salt and pepper, sprinkle in the sugar, and mix the filling thoroughly.

2 Place a spoonful of filling in the center of a wonton square. Bring the sides up, and press around the filling to make a basket shape. Flatten the base of the skin so that the wonton stands solid. The top should be wide open, exposing the filling.

3 Place the pockets on a heatproof plate, on a wire rack for a wok, or on the base of a cheesecloth-lined bamboo steamer.

Place over a wok, half-filled with boiling water, cover, then steam the pockets for about 20 minutes. Do this in 2 batches. Transfer to a warmed serving plate, sprinkle with toasted sesame seeds, drizzle with soy sauce, and serve immediately.

FOOD FACT

These steamed dumplings are known as *shao mai* in China, meaning "cook and sell," and are a popular street food. Serve them with a choice of dips, such as a sweet chili sauce, or a mixture of finely shredded ginger with a little honey, soy sauce, sesame oil, and rice vinegar or dry sherry.

TURKEY WITH ASIAN MUSHROOMS

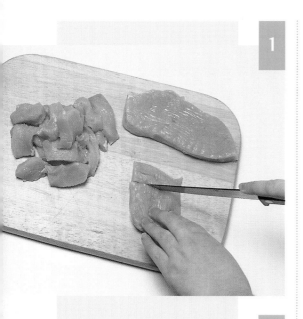

INGREDIENTS   Serves 4

½ cup dried Chinese
  mushrooms
1 lb. turkey breast steaks
⅔ cup turkey or chicken stock
2 tbsp. peanut oil
1 red bell pepper, deseeded
  and sliced
2 cups sugar snap peas,
  trimmed

¼ lb. shiitake mushrooms,
  wiped and halved
¼ lb. oyster mushrooms,
  wiped and halved
2 tbsp. yellow bean sauce
2 tbsp. soy sauce
1 tbsp. hot chili sauce
freshly cooked noodles, to
  serve

1 Place the dried mushrooms in a small bowl, cover with almost-boiling water, and leave for 20–30 minutes. Drain, and discard any woody stems from the mushrooms. Cut the turkey into thin strips.

2 Pour the turkey or chicken stock into a wok or large skillet, and bring to a boil. Add the turkey, and cook gently for 3 minutes or until the turkey is sealed completely. Then, using a slotted spoon, remove from the wok and set aside. Discard any stock.

3 Wipe the wok clean and reheat, then add the oil. When the oil is almost smoking, add the drained turkey and stir-fry for 2 minutes.

4 Add the drained mushrooms to the wok with the red bell

pepper, sugar snap peas, and shiitake and oyster mushrooms. Stir-fry for 2 minutes, then add the yellow bean, soy, and hot chili sauces.

5 Stir-fry the mixture for 1–2 minutes more or until the turkey is cooked thoroughly, and the vegetables are cooked, but still retain a bite. Turn into a warmed serving dish, and serve immediately with freshly cooked noodles.

HELPFUL HINT

Turkey is not normally associated with Chinese or Thai cuisine. However, it is now popular for its low-fat content and the many cuts that are available.

THAI GREEN FRAGRANT MUSSELS

INGREDIENTS   Serves 4

4½ lbs. fresh mussels

4 tbsp. olive oil

2 garlic cloves, peeled and
  finely sliced

3 tbsp. ginger, peeled and
  finely sliced

3 lemongrass stalks, outer
  leaves discarded and finely
  sliced

1–3 red or green chilies,
  deseeded and chopped

1 green bell pepper, deseeded
  and diced

5 scallions, trimmed and finely
  sliced

3 tbsp. freshly chopped
  cilantro

1 tbsp. sesame oil

juice of 3 limes

14-oz. can coconut milk

crusty bread, to serve

1 Scrub the mussels under cold running water, removing any barnacles and beards. Discard any that have broken or damaged shells, or are opened and do not close when tapped gently.

2 Heat a wok or large skillet, add the oil, and, when hot, add the mussels. Shake gently, and cook for 1 minute, then add the garlic, ginger, sliced lemongrass, chilies, green bell pepper, scallions, 2 tablespoons of the chopped cilantro, and the sesame oil.

3 Stir-fry over a medium heat for 3–4 minutes or until the mussels are cooked, and have opened. Discard any mussels that remain unopened.

4 Pour the lime juice and coconut milk into the wok, and bring to a boil. Tip the mussels and the cooking liquid into warmed individual bowls. Sprinkle with the remaining chopped cilantro and serve immediately with crusty bread.

HELPFUL HINT

Mussels and other shellfish are often eaten raw in Thailand. The less they are cooked, the better, as they will toughen and lose their fresh sea flavor if overcooked. Add the lime juice and coconut milk as soon as they have opened, and quickly bring to a boil. Buy mussels no more than 24 hours before you need them, so that they are really fresh.

GINGER LOBSTER

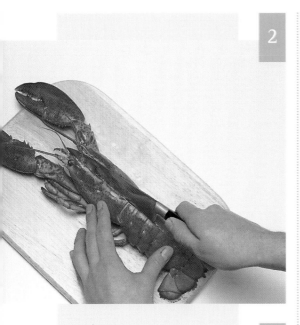

INGREDIENTS

Serves 4

1 celery stalk, trimmed and finely chopped

1 onion, peeled and chopped

1 small leek, trimmed and chopped

10 black peppercorns

1¼ lb. live lobster

2 tbsp. butter

½ cup peeled and finely chopped raw shrimp

6 tbsp. fish stock

⅓ cup ginger, peeled and thinly sliced

2 shallots, peeled and finely chopped

4 shiitake mushrooms, wiped and finely chopped

1 tsp. green peppercorns, drained and crushed

2 tbsp. oyster sauce

freshly ground black pepper

¼ tsp. cornstarch

sprigs of cilantro, to garnish

freshly cooked Thai rice and mixed shredded leek, celery, and red chili, to serve

1 Place the celery, onion, and leek in a large saucepan with the black peppercorns. Pour in 9 cups of hot water, bring to a boil, and boil for 5 minutes, then plunge the lobster into the water and boil for 8 minutes.

2 Remove the lobster. When cool enough to handle, turn it on its back. Using a sharp knife, halve the lobster neatly lengthwise. Remove and discard the intestinal vein from the tail, the stomach, (which lies near the head), and the inedible gills or dead man's fingers. Remove the meat from the shell and claws, and cut into pieces.

3 Heat a wok or large skillet, add the butter, and when melted, add the raw shrimp and fish stock. Stir-fry for 3 minutes or until the shrimp change color. Add the ginger, shallots, mushrooms, green peppercorns, and oyster sauce. Season to taste with black pepper. Stir in the lobster. Stir-fry for 2–3 minutes.

4 Blend the cornstarch with 1 teaspoon of water to form a thick paste, stir into the wok and cook, stirring, until the sauce thickens. Place the lobster on a warmed serving platter, and pour the sauce on top. Garnish and serve immediately.

HELPFUL HINT

Chilled or frozen lobster can be used instead of raw lobster. Omit cooking in Step 1, cut in half, and proceed as above.

CRISPY AROMATIC DUCK

INGREDIENTS   Serves 4–6

2 tbsp. Chinese five spice powder

3 oz. Szechuan peppercorns, lightly crushed

¼ cup black peppercorns, lightly crushed

3 tbsp. cumin seeds, lightly crushed

½ lb. rock salt

6 lb. oven-ready duck

3 inch piece fresh root ginger, peeled and cut into 6 slices

6 scallions, trimmed and cut into 3-in. lengths

cornstarch, for dusting

4 cups peanut oil

TO SERVE:

warm Chinese pancakes

spring onion, cut into shreds

cucumber, cut into slices lengthwise

hoisin sauce

1 Mix together the Chinese five spice powder, Szechuan and black peppercorns, cumin seeds, and salt. Rub the duck inside and out with the spice mixture. Wrap the duck in plastic wrap, and place in the refrigerator for 24 hours. Brush any loose spices from the duck. Place the ginger and scallions into the duck cavity, and put the duck on a heatproof plate.

2 Place a wire rack in a wok and pour in boiling water to a depth of 2 in. Place the duck on its plate on the rack, and cover. Steam gently for 2 hours or until the duck is cooked through. Pour off excess fat occasionally, and add more water if necessary. Remove the duck, pour off all the liquid, and discard the ginger and scallions. Leave the duck in a cool place for 2 hours or until it has dried and cooled.

3 Cut the duck into quarters, and dust lightly with cornstarch. Heat the oil in a wok or deep-fat fryer to 375° F, then deep-fry the duck quarters 2 at a time. Cook the breast quarters for 8–10 minutes and the thighs and legs for 12–14 minutes or until each piece is heated through. Drain on paper towels, then shred with a fork. Serve immediately with warm Chinese pancakes, scallion shreds, cucumber slices, and hoisin sauce.

TASTY TIP

To serve 4–6 people, you will need about 20 pancakes. Brush or spray each with a little water and a few drops of sesame oil. Layer them on a plate in a steamer, and warm through for 10 minutes.

SZECHUAN SESAME CHICKEN

INGREDIENTS   Serves 4

1 medium egg white
pinch of salt
2 tsp. cornstarch
1 lb. boneless, skinless
  chicken breast, cut into 3-in.
  strips
1¼ cups peanut oil
1 tbsp. sesame seeds
2 tsp. dark soy sauce
2 tsp. cider vinegar
2 tsp. chili bean sauce

2 tsp. sesame oil
2 tsp. sugar
1 tbsp. Chinese rice wine
1 tsp. whole Szechuan
  peppercorns, roasted
2 tbsp. trimmed and finely
  chopped scallion
mixed salad, to serve

1 Beat the egg white with a pinch of salt and the cornstarch, pour into a shallow dish, and add the chicken strips. Turn to coat, cover with plastic wrap, and leave in the refrigerator for 20 minutes.

2 Heat a wok, add the peanut oil, and, when hot, add the chicken pieces and stir-fry for 2 minutes or until the chicken turns white. Using a slotted spoon, remove the chicken and drain on paper towels. Pour off the oil, setting aside 1 tablespoon for stir-frying. Wipe the wok clean.

3 Reheat the wok, add the peanut oil with the sesame seeds, and stir-fry for 30 seconds or until golden. Stir in the dark soy sauce, cider vinegar, chili bean sauce, sesame oil, sugar, Chinese rice wine, Szechuan peppercorns, and the scallions. Bring to a boil.

4 Return the chicken to the wok, and stir-fry for 2 minutes, making sure that the chicken is evenly coated with the sauce and sesame seeds. Turn into a warmed serving dish, and serve immediately with a mixed salad.

FOOD FACT

Szechuan peppercorns, also known as "anise pepper," are the dried red berries of a type of ash tree. Hot and peppery, they are widely used in the spicy cuisine of the Szechuan region. They should always be roasted before use. If this has not already been done, place the berries on a baking tray, and roast in a preheated oven at 350° F for 15 minutes.

Shredded Chili Beef

INGREDIENTS

Serves 4

1 lb. lean steak, cut into very thin strips
1 tbsp. Chinese rice wine
1 tbsp. light soy sauce
2 tsp. sesame oil
2 tsp. cornstarch
8 red chilies, deseeded
8 garlic cloves, peeled
2 onions, peeled and sliced
1 tsp. Thai red curry paste
6 tbsp. peanut oil

2 red bell peppers, deseeded and sliced
2 celery stalks, trimmed and sliced
2 tbsp. Thai fish sauce
1 tbsp. dark soy sauce
shredded basil leaves and a sprig of fresh basil, to garnish
freshly cooked noodles, to serve

1 Place the beef in a bowl with the Chinese rice wine, light soy sauce, sesame oil, and cornstarch, and mix well. Cover with plastic wrap, and leave to marinate in the refrigerator for 20 minutes, turning the beef over at least once.

2 Place the chilies, garlic, onion, and red curry paste in a food processor, and blend to form a smooth paste.

3 Drain the beef, shaking off any excess marinade. Heat a wok and add 3 tablespoons of the peanut oil. When almost smoking, add the beef and stir-fry for 1 minute. Using a slotted spoon, remove the beef and set aside.

4 Wipe the wok clean, reheat, and add the remaining oil. When hot, add the chili paste and stir-fry for 30 seconds. Add the peppers, celery, fish sauce, and dark soy sauce. Stir-fry for 2 minutes. Return the beef to the wok and stir-fry for an additional 2 minutes or until the beef is cooked. Place in a warmed serving dish, sprinkle with shredded basil, add a basil sprig, and serve immediately with noodles.

TASTY TIP

This recipe contains a large amount of chilies as well as Thai red curry paste, but if you prefer a milder dish, reduce the quantity of chilies to 1 or 2. Choose regular red chilies rather than the tiny Thai ones, which make the dish extremely hot and fiery.

PORK WITH TOFU

INGREDIENTS   Serves 4

1 lb. smoked, firm tofu, drained
2 tbsp. peanut oil
3 garlic cloves, peeled and crushed
1-in. piece ginger, peeled and finely chopped
3/4 lb. fresh ground pork
1 tbsp. chili powder
1 tsp. sugar

2 tbsp. Chinese rice wine
1 tbsp. dark soy sauce
1 tbsp. light soy sauce
2 tbsp. yellow bean sauce
1 tsp. Szechuan peppercorns
5 tbsp. chicken stock
scallions, trimmed and finely sliced, to garnish
fried rice, to serve

1 Cut the tofu into ½-in. cubes, and place in a sieve to drain. Place the tofu on paper towels to dry thoroughly for an additional 10 minutes.

2 Heat the wok, add the peanut oil, and, when hot, add the garlic and ginger. Stir-fry for a few seconds to flavor the oil, but don't brown the vegetables. Add the ground pork and stir-fry for 3 minutes or until the pork is sealed and not clumping together in lumps.

3 Add all the remaining ingredients, except for the tofu. Bring the mixture to a boil, then reduce the heat to low. Add the tofu, and mix it in gently, taking care not to break up the chunks, but ensuring that the ingredients are evenly mixed. Simmer uncovered for 15 minutes or until the tofu is tender. Turn into a warmed serving dish, garnish with sliced scallions, and serve immediately with fried rice.

HELPFUL HINT

When adding spices, such as garlic and ginger, to hot oil, make sure you cook them for only a few seconds to develop their flavor. Move them around the pan all the time, and do not allow them to burn, or they will taste bitter. When adding the ground pork, break down the lumps of meat as much as possible.

ROYAL FRIED RICE

INGREDIENTS   Serves 4

1 lb. Thai fragrant rice
2 large eggs
2 tsp. sesame oil
salt and freshly ground black
  pepper
3 tbsp. vegetable oil
1 red bell pepper, deseeded
  and finely diced
1 yellow bell pepper, deseeded
  and finely diced
1 green bell pepper, deseeded
  and finely diced
2 red onions, peeled and diced

⅔ cup corn kernels
¾ cup peeled, cooked shrimp,
  thawed if frozen
½ cup white crabmeat, drained
  if canned
¼ tsp. sugar
2 tsp. light soy sauce

TO GARNISH:
radish roses
freshly cut and whole chives

1 Place the rice in a sieve, rinse with cold water, then drain. Place in a saucepan, and add twice the volume of water, stirring briefly. Bring to a boil, cover, and simmer gently for 15 minutes without stirring. If the rice has fully absorbed the water while covered, add a little more water. Continue to simmer uncovered for another 5 minutes or until the rice is fully cooked, and the water has evaporated. Let cool.

2 Place the eggs, sesame oil, and a pinch of salt in a bowl. Using a fork, mix just enough to break the egg. Set aside.

3 Heat a wok, and add 1 tablespoon of the vegetable oil. When very hot, stir-fry the bell peppers, onion, and corn for 2 minutes or until the onion is soft. Remove and set aside.

4 Clean the wok, and add the remaining oil. When very hot, add the cold cooked rice and stir-fry for 3 minutes or until it is heated through. Drizzle in the egg mixture, and continue to stir-fry for 2–3 minutes or until the eggs have set.

5 Add the shrimp and crabmeat to the rice. Stir-fry for 1 minute. Season to taste with salt and pepper, and add the sugar with the soy sauce. Stir to mix, and spoon into a warmed serving dish. Garnish with a radish flower, and sprinkle with freshly cut and whole chives. Serve immediately.

TASTY TIP

For more flavor, cook the rice in a light, unsalted chicken or vegetable stock.

CRISPY CHICKEN NOODLES

INGREDIENTS

Serves 4

1 medium egg white
2 tsp. cornstarch
salt and freshly ground white
  pepper
1¼ cups diced boneless and
  skinless chicken breast
½ lb. medium Chinese egg
  noodles
¾ cup peanut oil

2 tbsp. Chinese rice wine
2 tbsp. oyster sauce
1 tbsp. light soy sauce
1¼ cups chicken stock
1 tbsp. cornstarch

TO GARNISH:
scallion curls
toasted cashews

1 Mix the egg white with the cornstarch in a bowl, season to taste with salt and pepper, then add the chicken and stir to coat. Chill in the refrigerator for 20 minutes. Blanch the noodles for 2 minutes in a large saucepan of boiling salted water, and drain.

2 Heat a wok or large skillet and add 2 tablespoons of the peanut oil. When hot, spread the noodles evenly over the surface, reduce the heat to low, and cook for about 5 minutes, or until browned on one side. Gently turn over, adding extra oil if necessary, and cook until both sides are browned. Set aside and keep warm.

3 Drain the chicken. Wipe the wok clean, reheat, and add the remaining peanut oil. When hot, add the chicken and stir-fry for 2 minutes. Using a slotted spoon, remove, and drain on paper towels. Keep warm.

4 Wipe the wok clean, reheat, and pour in the Chinese rice wine, oyster sauce, soy sauce, and chicken stock, and season lightly. Bring to a boil. Blend the cornstarch to a paste with 2 tablespoons of water, and stir into the wok. Cook, stirring, until the sauce has thickened. Cook for an additional minute.

5 Tip the noodles onto warmed plates, top with the crispy chicken pieces, and drizzle with the sauce. Garnish with scallion curls, and sprinkle with toasted cashews. Serve immediately.

TASTY TIP

Tossing chicken in a mixture of egg whites and cornstarch creates a protective crispy coating that keeps it succulent.

STIR-FRIED GREENS

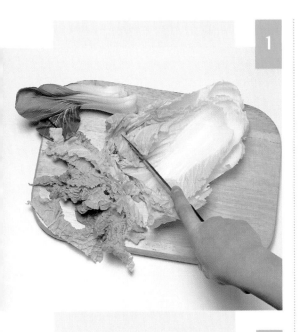

INGREDIENTS   Serves 4

1 lb. Chinese cabbage
½ lb. bok choy
2 cups broccoli florets
1 tbsp. sesame seeds
1 tbsp. peanut oil
1 tbsp. fresh ginger, peeled
  and finely chopped
3 garlic cloves, peeled and
  finely chopped
2 red chilies, deseeded and
  split in half
¼ cup chicken stock
2 tbsp. Chinese rice wine

1 tbsp. dark soy sauce
1 tsp. light soy sauce
2 tsp. black bean sauce
freshly ground black pepper
2 tsp. sugar
1 tsp. sesame oil

1 Separate the Chinese cabbage and bok choy into leaves, and wash well. Cut into 1-in. strips. Separate the broccoli into small florets. Heat a wok or large skillet, add the sesame seeds, and stir-fry for 30 seconds.

2 Add the oil to the wok, and, when hot, add the ginger, garlic, and chilies, and stir-fry for 30 seconds. Add the broccoli and stir-fry for 1 minute. Add the Chinese cabbage and bok choy, and stir-fry for an additional 1 minute.

3 Pour the chicken stock, Chinese rice wine, and the soy and black bean sauces into the wok. Season to taste with pepper, and add the sugar. Reduce the heat and simmer for 6–8 minutes or until the vegetables are tender but still firm to the bite. Tip into a warmed serving dish, removing the chilies, if desired. Drizzle with the sesame oil, and serve immediately.

FOOD FACT

Sugar is an ingredient which is often used in Chinese and Thai cooking to round out and balance flavors. Combined with vinegar, as here, it gives a sweet-and-sour flavor. Palm sugar is often used as it has a slight caramel taste, and adds a golden-brown color to dishes. You can buy it from Asian markets, either in packages or cans. Golden brown or raw sugar can also be used.

COLORFUL BEEF IN LETTUCE

INGREDIENTS   Serves 4

1 lb. ground beef
2 tbsp. Chinese rice wine
1 tbsp. light soy sauce
2 tsp. sesame oil
2 tsp. cornstarch
1 cup Chinese dried
  mushrooms
2 tbsp. peanut oil
1 garlic clove, peeled and
  crushed
1 shallot, peeled and finely
  chopped
2 scallions, trimmed and finely
  sliced
2 carrots, peeled and thinly
  sliced

½ cup canned bamboo shoots,
  thinly sliced
2 zucchini, trimmed and thinly
  sliced
1 red bell pepper, deseeded
  and thinly sliced
1 tbsp. dark soy sauce
2 tbsp. hoisin sauce
2 tbsp. oyster sauce
4 large iceberg lettuce leaves
sprigs of fresh Italian parsley,
  to garnish

1 Place the ground steak in a bowl with 1 tablespoon of the Chinese rice wine, light soy sauce, sesame oil, and cornstarch. Mix well, and leave for 20 minutes.

2 Soak the dried mushrooms in almost-boiling water for 20 minutes. Drain, rinse, drain again, and squeeze out excess liquid. Trim and slice finely.

3 Heat a wok or large skillet, add 1 tablespoon of the peanut oil, and, when very hot, add the beef. Stir-fry for 1 minute, then remove using a slotted spoon. Set aside.

4 Wipe the wok clean and reheat. Add the remaining oil, and, when hot, add the garlic, shallot, and scallions, and stir-fry for 10 seconds. Add the carrots and stir-fry for 1 minute. Add the mushrooms, bamboo shoots, zucchini, and pepper, and stir-fry for 1 minute. Add the steak, soy, and hoisin and oyster sauces to the wok, and stir-fry for 3 minutes.

5 Spoon the beef mixture onto lettuce leaves, and fold into pockets. Garnish with Italian parsley, and serve.

HELPFUL HINT

Use a good-quality ground beef, and fry it over a high heat so that it browns well.

COCONUT SORBET WITH MANGO SAUCE

INGREDIENTS
Serves 4

2 sheets gelatin
1½ cups superfine sugar
2½ cups coconut milk

2 mangos, peeled, pitted, and sliced
2 tbsp. confectioners' sugar
zest and juice of 1 lime

1 Place the sheets of gelatin in a shallow dish, cover with cold water, and leave for 15 minutes. Drain and squeeze out excess moisture.

2 Meanwhile, place the superfine sugar and 1¼ cups of the coconut milk in a heavy-based saucepan, and heat gently, stirring occasionally, until the sugar has dissolved. Remove from the heat.

3 Add the soaked gelatin to the saucepan, and stir gently until dissolved. Stir in the remaining coconut milk. Let cool.

4 Pour the gelatin and coconut mixture into a freezer container, and place in the freezer. Leave for at least 1 hour or until ice crystals have started to form around the edge of the mixture. Remove and beat with a spoon, then return to the freezer, and continue to freeze until the mixture is frozen, beating at least twice more during this time.

5 Meanwhile, make the sauce. Place the sliced mango, confectioners' sugar, and the lime zest and juice in a food processor, and blend until smooth. Spoon into a small pitcher.

6 Leave the sorbet to soften in the refrigerator for at least 30 minutes before serving. Serve scoops of sorbet on individual plates with a little of the mango sauce poured on top.

HELPFUL HINT

The gelatin helps prevent large, gritty ice crystals from forming as the sorbet freezes, giving it a smoother, creamier texture. You can use powdered gelatin if you prefer. Sprinkle 2 level teaspoons over 2 tablespoons of cold water, leave for 5 minutes, then stir into the hot coconut milk at the beginning of Step 3.

ROSE-WATER DOUGH BALLS WITH YOGURT SAUCE

INGREDIENTS   Makes 30

2¾ cups self-rising flour, sifted	scant ½ cup superfine sugar
½ cup ground almonds	lime zest, to decorate
⅓ cup butter, cubed	
5 tbsp. natural yogurt	**FOR THE YOGURT SAUCE:**
2 tsp. rose water	¾ cup plain yogurt
grated zest of 1 orange	2 tsp. rose water
2½ cups vegetable oil	grated zest of 1 lime
	1 tbsp. confectioners' sugar

1 To make the yogurt sauce, blend the yogurt with the rose water and lime zest in a small bowl. Sift in the confectioners' sugar and mix. Pour into a serving pitcher, cover with plastic wrap, and refrigerate until ready to serve.

2 Place the flour and ground almonds in a large bowl, and, using your fingertips, rub in the butter until the mixture resembles fine bread crumbs.

3 Add the yogurt, rose water, and orange zest to the crumb mixture, pour in ¼ cup of warm water, and mix with a knife to form a soft, pliable dough. Turn onto a lightly floured board, and knead for 2 minutes or until smooth, then divide the dough into 30 small balls.

4 Heat the vegetable oil in a large wok or deep-fat fryer to 375° F. Working in small batches, deep-fry the dough balls for 5–6 minutes or until golden brown. Using a slotted spoon, remove the balls from the oil, and drain on paper towels.

5 Pour the superfine sugar on a plate, and roll all the dough balls in the sugar until well coated. Decorate with a little lime zest, and serve immediately with the yogurt sauce.

FOOD FACT

Rose water is a clear, fragrant liquid, distilled from rose petals or from rose oil. It is the flavoring used in Turkish delight. Use it sparingly, as it is very powerful. Orange flower water, distilled from the flowers of Seville oranges, also works well here.

CHOCOLATE & LEMONGRASS MOUSSE

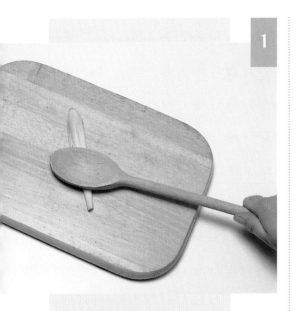

INGREDIENTS Serves 4

3 lemongrass stalks, outer
   leaves removed
¾ cup milk
2 sheets gelatin
5 squares milk chocolate,
   broken into small pieces

2 medium egg yolks
⅓ cup superfine sugar
⅔ cup heavy cream
juice of 2 lemons
1 tbsp. superfine sugar
lemon zest, to decorate

1 Use a wooden spoon to bruise the lemongrass, then cut in half. Pour the milk into a large, heavy-based saucepan, add the lemongrass, and bring to a boil. Remove from the heat, leave for 1 hour, then strain. Place the gelatin in a shallow dish, pour over cold water to cover, and leave for 15 minutes. Drain and squeeze out excess moisture.

2 Place the chocolate in a small bowl set over a saucepan of gently simmering water, and leave until melted. Make sure the water does not touch the bowl.

3 Whisk the egg yolks and sugar together until thick, then whisk in the flavored milk. Pour into a clean saucepan, and cook gently, stirring continuously, until the mixture starts to thicken. Remove from the heat, stir in the melted chocolate and gelatin, and let cool for a few minutes.

4 Whisk the heavy cream until soft peaks form, then stir into the cooled milk mixture to make a mousse. Spoon into individual ramekins or molds, and refrigerate until set.

5 Just before serving, pour the lemon juice into a small saucepan, bring to a boil, then simmer for 3 minutes or until reduced. Add the sugar, and heat until dissolved, stirring continuously. Serve the mousse drizzled with the lemon sauce and decorated with lemon zest.

HELPFUL HINT

Take care not to overheat milk chocolate when melting it— the water in the pan should barely be bubbling; it is a good idea to turn off the heat as soon as the chocolate begins to melt. Buy baking chocolate, but avoid chocolate-flavored cake covering.

COCONUT RICE SERVED WITH STEWED GINGER FRUITS

INGREDIENTS

Serves 6–8

1 vanilla pod
2 cups coconut milk
5 cups low-fat milk
2½ cups heavy cream
⅔ cup superfine sugar
2 star anise
8 tbsp. toasted dried coconut
1½ cups short-grain pudding
   rice
1 tsp. melted butter

2 mandarin oranges, peeled
   and pith removed
1 carambola or star fruit,
   sliced
⅓ cup finely diced, preserved
   ginger
1¼ cups sweet white wine
superfine sugar, to taste

1 Preheat the oven to 325° F. Using a sharp knife, split the vanilla pod in half lengthwise, scrape out the seeds from the pods, and place both the pod and seeds in a large, heavy-based casserole dish. Pour in the coconut milk, low-fat milk, and heavy cream, and stir in the sugar, star anise, and 4 tablespoons of the toasted coconut. Bring to a boil, then simmer for 10 minutes, stirring occasionally. Remove the vanilla pod and star anise.

2 Wash the rice and add to the milk. Simmer gently for 25–30 minutes or until the rice is tender, stirring frequently. Stir in the melted butter.

3 Divide the mandarins into segments, and place in a saucepan with the sliced carambola or star fruit and stem ginger. Pour in the wine and 1¼ cups water, bring to a boil, then reduce the heat, and simmer for 20 minutes or until the liquid has reduced and the fruits softened. Add sugar to taste.

4 Serve the rice topped with the stewed fruits and the remaining toasted coconut.

FOOD FACT

Star fruit, or carambola, is a pale yellow-green fruit with a pretty star-shaped appearance when cut horizontally. It is almost flavorless, with just a hint of sweet and sour, and has a crunchy texture when eaten raw. Poaching it in white wine and ginger enhances its light flavor.

PASSION FRUIT & POMEGRANATE CITRUS TART

INGREDIENTS   Serves 4

FOR THE PASTRY:
1½ cups all-purpose flour
pinch of salt
½ cup butter
4 tsp. superfine sugar
1 small egg, separated

FOR THE FILLING:
2 passion fruit
1 cup superfine sugar
4 large eggs
¾ cup heavy cream
3 tbsp. lime juice
1 pomegranate
confectioners' sugar, for dusting

1 Preheat the oven to 400° F. Sift the flour and salt into a large bowl, and rub in the butter until the mixture resembles fine bread crumbs. Stir in the sugar.

2 Whisk the egg yolk, and add to the dry ingredients. Mix well to form a smooth, pliable dough. Knead gently on a lightly floured surface until smooth. Wrap the pastry, and let rest in the refrigerator for 30 minutes.

3 Roll out the pastry on a lightly floured surface, and use to line a 10-in. loose-based tart pan. Line the pastry shell with waxed paper and baking beans. Brush the edges of the pastry with the egg white, and bake blind in the preheated oven for 15 minutes. Remove the paper and beans, and bake for 5 minutes. Remove, and reduce the oven temperature to 350° F.

4 Halve the passion fruit and spoon the flesh into a bowl. Whisk the sugar and eggs together in a bowl. When mixed thoroughly, stir in the heavy cream, the passion fruit juice and flesh, and the lime juice.

5 Pour the mixture into the pastry shell, and bake for 30–40 minutes or until the filling is just set. Remove and cool slightly, then chill in the refrigerator for 1 hour. Cut the pomegranate in half and scoop the seeds into a sieve. Spoon the drained seeds over the tart, and dust with confectioners' sugar just before serving.

HELPFUL HINT
Pomegranates have a leathery skin and may be dark yellow to crimson in color. They have a distinctive, slightly acidic flavor.

INDEX